Advance praise for *Corporate Culture/Team Culture:*

"A bellwether book in today's tumultuous and competitive environment. It provides a practical model to help with the 'human' side of mergers, acquisitions, and change. Every manager and every organization can benefit from the message."

—Alan Lam, Vice President, Chase Manhattan Bank, N.A.

"So simple, yet so profound! This book provides eye-opening truths for making the dramatic cultural shifts needed in most organizations. It captures the essence of what is not working in organizations and offers invaluable wisdom and advice on the remedy."

—Suresh C. Chugh, Managing Director, J. P. Morgan

"A very practical guide on how to make lasting change take root in an organization by impacting its culture. Full of examples that vividly illustrate how to harness the power of teams to drive performance improvement."

—Peter M. Paolucci, Vice President-Sales, Shell Chemical Company

"The process described in Sherriton and Stern's book is a great tool for guiding corporate culture change to one supporting and nourishing effective teamwork."

—Keld Alstrup, Vice President, International Human Resources, AB Volvo

"*Corporate Culture/Team Culture* gives every CEO a clear and concise blueprint for building a successful organization. It's an interesting read, full of succinct examples and distinct models that offer clear direction on making any business a more productive, effective, and pleasant place to work."

—Fred D. Hirt, President and CEO
Mount Sinai Medical Center of Greater Miami

"This is a must read for every manager and employee grappling with changing an organization's culture."

—Enrique Martinez, Vice President-Regional Director
Latin America Rohm & Haas

"*Corporate Culture/Team Culture* is *the* guide to effecting culture change. Sherriton and Stern are giving organizations the tools to harness the creative powers of the entire organization. The guidelines they provide will enable management to implement culture change in a seamless manner."

—Patrick O'Malley, Director of Operations, Planters Company

"Provides a step-by-step approach to assure team success, including a model for facilitating culture change. This is a must read for companies undergoing the transition to a team-based culture."

—Jerome Birnbaum, Ph.D., Senior Vice President
Bristol-Myers Squibb Pharmaceutical Research Institute

"This book is right on target. I have personally used the transitional process to create a team culture in the companies I have had to 'turn around.' The financial result was sales growth substantially greater than the industry average, which resulted in dramatic profit growth. I recommend this book to anyone who wants to make a difference while simultaneously having fun."

—Timothy J. Loncharich, President and CEO, Snelling Personnel Services

"The fundamental approaches and model described in *Corporate Culture/Team Culture* really made a difference to our Sales and Services Quality and Information Technology Organization. They were able to focus organizational commitment and accelerate movement to a team-oriented structure that boosted cross-organizational resource sharing, vitality, and achievement of business results."

—Jill Kanin-Lovers, Vice President Human Resources, USA, IBM

Corporate Culture Team Culture

Removing the Hidden Barriers to Team Success

Jacalyn Sherriton
& James L. Stern

amacom

American Management Association

New York • Atlanta • Boston • Chicago • Kansas City • San Francisco • Washington, D.C.
Brussels • Mexico City • Tokyo • Toronto

This publication is designed to provide accurate and authoritative
information in regard to the subject matter covered. It is sold with the
understanding that the publisher is not engaged in rendering legal,
accounting, or other professional service. If legal advice or other expert
assistance is required, the services of a competent professional person
should be sought.

Library of Congress Cataloging-in-Publication Data

Sherriton, Jacalyn Carol.
    Corporate culture, team culture : removing the hidden barriers to
team success / Jacalyn Sherriton & James L. Stern.
        p.   cm.
    Includes index.
    ISBN 0-8144-0324-7
    1. Work groups.   2. Corporate culture.   I. Stern, James L.
II. Title.
HD66.S486   1996
658.4'02—dc20   96-24403
                                                              CIP

Printing number

10   9   8   7   6   5   4

Contents

Preface

As management consultants, we spend our time traveling from organization to organization helping corporations face up to the challenges of today's changing business environment. The changes these corporations face are truly daunting, and meeting them requires dramatic efforts. In fact, we feel that a virtual cultural revolution is needed to transform today's companies to a formal team environment.

But how can companies achieve this ambitious end? We pondered this many years ago when one evening we found ourselves seated over a long dinner discussing some of the recurring themes and strategies we'd come across and used in our work. By dinner's end, we had formulated the broad outlines of what has become our Organization Culture Change Model. We've since used this model in a variety of organizations, and have watched it evolve as we learned valuable lessons through helping companies make their sometimes difficult transitions to the use of formal teams.

In both our consulting practice and our nationwide speaking engagements, we've been bombarded with requests for "our book"—something we did not have until now. We hope that this book will satisfy our clients' and audiences' requests by introducing them to our Change Model (the fruit of that long-ago dinner) and helping them along the culture-change journey that their organizations are embarking on.

Acknowledgments

Most of the material for this book came from our collective consulting experience. That means, of course, that the relationships we've developed with our clients have had a major influence on our thoughts and perspective. These relationships with executives, managers, and the workforce in our client organizations really guided the direction of the book. We would like to acknowledge them collectively.

A special thank-you goes to our clients in the following organizations, who were determined and courageous in taking on a change of culture or subculture to support their team construct:

- IBM Quality and Information Technology
- Mobil Oil Corporation's Research and Engineering departments of the past and the current Mobil Technology Company and Shared Security Services
- Bristol-Myers Squibb
- AMI Semiconductors
- Rohm & Haas
- Attorneys' Title Insurance Fund
- U.S. Food and Drug Administration
- The *Fort Lauderdale Sun-Sentinel*

The impetus for writing this book really came from many of our colleagues, friends, and family members. Their suggestions, and sometimes their insistence, that we capture and share the work we've done provided the drive we needed to move forward. For that drive, impetus, and encouragement, we are sincerely grateful.

Also, we owe special thanks to our development editor, Jacqueline Laks Gorman, whose good humor and positive outlook helped us through some difficult times.

An extra measure of thanks goes to Adrienne Hickey, senior acquisitions editor at AMACOM, for recognizing the value of our book.

To our families, thank you for encouraging us to fully appreciate, respect, and utilize differences among people and cultures.

Last, but most of all, we want to thank each other as partners in business as well as in this endeavor. We've worked well as a partnership, sometimes under very stressful circumstances, in climbing this "personal mountain." And the team survives!

1

The Challenge and Meeting It

The art of progress is to preserve order amid change and to preserve change amid order.

—Alfred North Whitehead

Businesspeople today are the first to admit that American businesses are facing the greatest, most traumatic changes in their history. These changes include:

- The need to become global in focus and operations
- The specter of downsizing or rightsizing
- The advent of reengineering
- The complexities of mergers and acquisitions
- The need to remain competitive amid all this change

The resulting demand on employees to become more efficient—to do more with less—has created a real need to rethink the fundamentals of how work in any company gets done. The need is reinforced by the challenge of coordinating highly diversified and specialized functions within an organization being wrenched into change for the sake of survival.

The Move to Formal Teams

For many companies, large and small, this rethinking has led to the very practical conclusion that the answer is to have employees work in formal teams. The key is the word *formal*. Every organization has some history of engaging in teamwork. Most have touted it, even encouraged it, while some have only allowed or tolerated teamwork. In this ad hoc team environment of the past, employees came together informally to generate ideas or solve problems. These teams were not considered a formal part of the organizational structure and were seldom recognized in formal compensation or reward systems. But the organization would opt for teamwork when a contribution was required from various groups across an organization.

Faced with new challenges, organizations today are quickly moving toward new, formal structures where cross-functional teaming replaces the traditional hierarchical organization with a matrix structure. Short-term, long-term, and even permanent alliances among functions or across organizations are prevalent. Interdisciplinary and interdepartmental project teams are becoming the norm in how work gets done. Federal Express, for example, automatically forms a team to address any issue that arises. It's just the way the company operates.

Many company leaders believe this transition to formalizing teams is simple. They send out a few memos, meet with employees to explain briefly how and why teams are important, make some adjustments to the organization's structure, train all employees, and there they are! "Now," they think, "we're operating in teams." If only it *were* so simple.

Instead, the transition from the traditional company, characterized by hierarchy and command and control, to one based on teams is a long, difficult journey. The very concept of teams goes against the mind-sets and systems in place within society and many of our organizations. In fact, we have found that many employees don't even like informal team environments. Given all this, the move to formal teams must be treated as a major change in an organization's culture.

The notion of changing the culture of an organization to

employ teams effectively is alien to most companies. Most leaders and managers assume either that the culture will take care of itself or that it must already support any concept as ideal as that of teamwork. Since culture is an unspoken, habitual way of doing things, it is typically not dissected or analyzed. Thus, how well an organization's culture truly supports the formalized concept of teams is often misunderstood or neglected.

In our experience, changing organizational culture is the only way to provide some assurance that formalization of teams will be successful. There must be a conscious process to assess and change the culture to support teams and teamwork. Too many organizations fail to recognize this and lose precious time, productivity, and money on unsuccessful team efforts.

They can't afford to do this. The traumatic changes being faced by America's businesses are only in their beginning stages, and both the current and predicted shakeouts in many industries increase the need for companies to become more efficient and more flexible. The future requires greater use of new teams and more creative use of existing teams. It is critical that businesses make a successful transition to an environment that supports teams and teamwork.

The Challenge Is Change

The Washington Post of December 14, 1995, reported at least four large mergers/acquisitions involving American companies: Litton Industries, DuPont, Campbell Soup, and Bristol-Myers Squibb. This is just on one normal day in the current business world.

Mergers/acquisitions are rampant, and there is no letup in sight. According to Mergerstat, a merger research service, deals worth over $248 billion were made in the first three quarters of 1995.[1] Mergers/acquisitions are usually designed to produce synergism between the participating companies and overall cost reduction through economies of scale. In each deal, the merging of the companies means the ultimate merging of critical functions within companies, such as distribution systems, marketing programs, sales organizations, or manufacturing facilities.

Globalization is another factor. L'Oreal, a French company, recently announced a merger with the third largest U.S. cosmetics firm, Maybelline. Another example is Matsushita's acquiring MCA a few years ago and the recent spinoff of MCA to Seagram. In these cross-border deals, a company has to cope not only with the corporate culture issues but with the added issues of national culture mixes.

Many organizations have found that the mergers/acquisitions route is fraught with problems, and they have sought a less permanent, less complex strategy to achieve the expected synergy. This has led to strategic alliances. Partnering in more focused and specific ways makes sense to many organizations. Texas Instruments and Hitachi formed an alliance to develop new memory chips and are jointly building a new manufacturing plant in Dallas. U.S. West and Tele-Communications, Inc. (TCI), have formed a joint venture in Great Britain to provide telephone and cable services. Many major oil companies have been forming joint ventures to share technology and oil reserves to make exploration and production more efficient.

Alliances are also common in the health care industry. Physicians in private practices are aligning with hospitals, and hospitals are aligning with each other to reduce duplication in services and equipment. In addition, integrated networks are being formed through alliances to provide a continuum of care, from primary to long-term and nursing home care.

Perhaps the greatest impact on American business today is the advent of downsizing (or rightsizing, or any of a number of euphemisms for layoffs) as a survival strategy. Foreign and domestic companies in every industry find their bottom lines adversely affected by increasing costs for personnel, raw materials, real estate, and equipment. At the same time, prices for products and services are being driven down by competition, new technology, and increased productivity. This new environment of keener competition has prompted companies to cut their costs in order to remain competitive—indeed, to survive. As a result, over the past five years organizations have been shedding employees at a frantic rate. IBM has reduced its workforce by close to 50 percent in three waves. Mobil Oil has pared down by about 30 percent. AT&T has already taken huge cuts and has announced cutting 40,000 more. It's difficult to find a company that has not attempted a cutback strategy of some kind. Even the federal government is "reinventing" itself and is cutting back by more than 200,000 workers.

Reengineering is another strategy of late. What business is there that *hasn't* engaged in some attempt to reengineer its processes to become as efficient and effective as possible? Reengineering initiatives deal with rethinking *how* work gets done, and not just doing it faster and harder.

And, of course, there is Total Quality Management (TQM), a movement that has swept into government and industry and created a dramatic stir in most organizations. TQM is about change in how we act, think, do work, and structure our organizations.

All of these strategies have been implemented to make organizations more competitive. But how well is all this working?

Is the Remedy Worse Than the Illness?

These drastic remedies have resulted in a scaled-back workforce of survivors who are overworked and stressed out, and who feel set adrift in organizations without the safety and security anchors of the past. People are working longer hours under reduced benefits. Strat Sherman writes in *Fortune*: "We all agree that generally you get more output by committing more input, but now corporate America seems to be trying to get more output just by demanding more output."[2]

The synergy and/or cost reductions envisioned for mergers aren't always realized. Companies tend to spend millions of dollars to analyze the financials of deals, only to have them fail because they haven't accounted for the issues that nearly always arise when two dissimilar corporate cultures are merged. Anne B. Fisher writes in *Fortune* that the most successful mergers are those in which managers take time to understand thoroughly what they're getting into and are willing to build a new culture that makes use of the best from both partners. She compares companies with clashing styles in a merger to a miserably married couple living as strangers under the same roof.[3]

A case in point might be the ill-fated acquisition of MCA by Matsushita of Japan. Matsushita spent a number of turbulent years trying to "adapt" MCA's entertainment-oriented, creative, freewheeling Hollywood culture to Matsushita's own more staid, risk-averse, bottom-line-oriented Japanese culture but finally sold MCA to Seagram.

Alliances, too, have run into some trouble. Take Kaleida Labs, the software joint venture formed in 1991 by Apple Computer and IBM. After engineers from the two companies continued to haggle over job responsibilities, the joint venture was scrapped in late 1995.[4] Here is a clear example of two incompatible cultures not meshing to realize the synergy expected from the alliance. There are numerous similar examples in the health care industry, where poorly conceived, poorly planned alliances have not reaped the expected benefits.

And, of course, the TQM fad for most organizations ended the way many previous fads have: in princely expenditures for a pauper's returns.

In short, organizations today are using numerous strategies to make themselves more competitive and to ensure their survival. These strategies are working for some but not for others. One of the major contributors to success or failure lies in the implementation of the strategy and the way organizations make dissimilar cultures compatible.

Meeting the Challenge

In looking at how companies are trying to meet the challenges posed by today's business environment, we have found that the most typical response involves the increased use of teams in accomplishing work. Organizations are discovering that with reduced workforces, but usually no reduction in the work itself, they must change how they do things. A major way to do so is through the use of teams. A study on managing organizational change in Florida, done by the Fort Lauderdale company Right Associates, indicated that team-oriented work approaches are an outgrowth of restructuring and downsizing. The report showed that 81 percent of the organizations studied have shifted work across traditional boundaries, and that there is a strong trend toward teams and away from hierarchical departments.[5]

The mergers/acquisitions and alliance strategies have also dictated the need for the newly merged and aligned organizations to embrace the tenets of teams. Successfully meshing these organizations into teams that can meet the established goals is the point of the strategy, after all. The hope and expectation is to have an "organization team" where branches, divisions, and departments from dissimilar cultures come together in synergy. In addition, TQM and reengineering both espouse the use of teams to accomplish work. In the case of TQM, the focus is on use of a teaming concept to formalize the quality process.

The implementation of all these strategies is being translated to a real trend toward teams and teaming in more formalized structures. *The Wall Street Journal* reported on April 12, 1995, that 67 percent of large American companies assign some workers to teams, compared with 28 percent in 1987. A 1994 survey sponsored by the Society for Human Resources Management and CCH, Inc., found that 86 percent of companies surveyed report developing cross-functional teams, and 64 percent self-directed work teams.[6]

Even Wall Street respects the trend toward teams. A study by the California Public Employees' Retirement System showed that companies that involve employees in decision making boast stronger market valuations than those that don't. *USA Today* advised investors to look for companies that attempt "to motivate employees to work as a team." The newspaper quoted management consultant William Dunk: "For companies to win more business with fewer employees, those employees are going to have to play together like a symphony."[7]

So teams and teaming are upon us and are here to stay. But even though the need for teams is clear and the desire for teams is high, most organizations don't do a good job of formalizing the team concept and integrating teams into the existing culture.

As previously stated, one reason why mergers, acquisitions, alliances, TQM, and restructuring don't always work is that companies don't fully consider the implications for their corporate or organizational cultures. This is also the case with the use of formalized teams that result from those strategies. If teaming is the preferred method used to implement these competitive strategies, then some preparation of the organization's culture to accept and thrive in a teaming environment is necessary. As writer Brian Dumaine notes, teams often get launched in a vacuum, with little or no training or support. There may be no changes in the design of work and no change in overall practices, such as reward systems.[8] Organizations that implement teams halfheartedly will find their efforts doomed to fail.

Corporate Culture/Team Culture

Clearly, the change to teams must be addressed as an overall change in culture. There is an obvious need for a specific methodology to address changing an organization's culture. The trend toward teams has fostered a proliferation of books and other publications written for teams and about teamwork. There are hundreds of sources providing information on teams, but virtually none on preparing the organization's culture to accept and support formal teaming. As an outgrowth of our research and actual consulting work with many of the companies discussed herein, this book provides that information. It is about corporate culture: changing it or creating it. It makes the case that this change in or creation of corporate culture is a requisite for the successful implementation of formal teams in today's organizations.

The book is specifically designed to help the reader assess the need for culture change in his/her own organization. That organization may be an entire company, agency, or not-for-profit association, or it could be a subordinate but integral part of the overall organization, for example a division, department, or branch where a subculture to the overall corporate culture is in need of change. The book is thus directed to managers and leaders at all levels in organizations that are currently involved with or are entertaining the idea of increasing their use of and reliance on teams, as well as those who are dealing with current or potential mergers, acquisitions, or alliances. This book is a primer for changing the organizational culture. It is for organization leaders who are experiencing the pitfalls and difficulties of attempting to institutionalize teams in their organizations and who need to understand and overcome the unexpected traumas they are encountering.

The methods described have been successfully used in changing the overall culture of companies when employed by the senior executive team and successive levels of management. But changing the overall culture is only one facet. Even more important are the thousands of midlevel managers—vice-presidents, division managers, and department managers—who find themselves in the less-than-ideal position of having to make teams work within their own subcultures. Many of these managers are experiencing tremendous frustration with the existing corporate culture and the lack of support and/or understanding they are getting from the senior executive level. These managers now have a source to guide them through changing their subculture, to ensure their own success with teams. The current management theory is that to change culture, executive-level support is mandatory and all systems *throughout* the company must be in alignment. However, this book describes successful change in subcultures when top-level support and alignment were absent or sporadic. It gives strategies for success to managers in similar situations.

How This Book Is Organized

The chapters that follow make the case for corporate culture (or subculture) being the critical link in the transition to teamwork. Chapter 2 identifies what is going wrong in the current implementation of formalized teams. It describes various hierarchical perspectives as well as the most frequently encountered organizational and team issues that hinder success. The chapter discusses typical strategies and myths related to changing corporate culture and teams/teamwork, and it highlights key ingredients for successful implementation that are most frequently missing.

Chapter 3 emphasizes the importance of having a corporate culture that supports formalized teams. It defines corporate culture and explains its distinction from subcultures. The chapter also examines possible reasons why corporate culture is often neglected and not part of the change process. We describe various aspects of a corporate culture that can support or hinder implementation of teams.

Chapter 4 provides a general overview of how you begin to stimulate culture change. It contrasts the ideal option (change from the top) with one that is practical and more realistic for many managers (change from the middle). The requirements for creating a supportive culture for teaming are explored from numerous angles. These include issues related to transitioning traditional cultures and senior and midlevel manager styles, planning, empowerment, overcoming cultural barriers such as the team concept's being antithetical to societal and organizational values, and resource requirements for the change.

Chapter 5 discusses in general why the Organization Culture Change Model was developed for changing culture to support teamwork. It introduces the model and describes the experiences of a number of organizations that used it to change their cultures. The discussion raises the issue of using the model to change the overall culture of an entire company and introduces the means and methods of changing a subculture within an overall company's corporate culture.

Chapters 6 through 11 then dissect the model into its component parts and describe each. The description of each component includes examples of how it has been applied in a variety of organizations.

Chapter 12 pulls it all together and asks you to reflect on the degree to which you feel empowered to create your own culture or subculture. It discusses the leader's role in moving the organization forward. This final chapter also gives the results of culture change efforts in real companies.

This book does provide the recipes and ingredients for accomplishing organizational culture change. However, no book can provide the expertise and experience that are often necessary to be fully successful in such a complex endeavor. The successful experiences described in this book resulted from the methodology outlined here. These successes came in no small part through leaders and managers who acted as champions for change and who became aware of and understood what was required to succeed.

There is one caution to the reader. Although this book gives the recipes and ingredients, the leaders who managed the successes described here enlisted the support and guidance of experts in the art and science of large-scale organizational culture change. These experts were sometimes internal human resources professionals, and oftentimes external organizational development consultants. This book is also useful to those internal and external professionals versed in culture change for organizations.

For both the leaders and managers and their supporting players, this book is designed to ease the transition to teams through culture change by reducing the risk and increasing the opportunity for success.

Notes

1. Phillip L. Zweig, "The Case Against Mergers," *Business Week*, October 30, 1995.

2. Strat Sherman, "Stretch Goals: The Dark Side of Asking for Miracles," *Fortune*, November 13, 1995.

3. Anne B. Fisher, "How to Make a Merger Work," *Fortune*, January 24, 1994.

4. "Kaleida Labs Calls It Quits," *Business Week*, December 4, 1995.

5. "Managing Change in Florida," research study by Right Associates, Fort Lauderdale, 1995.

6. Ninth Annual Society for Human Resources Management/CCH, Inc., Survey, 1994.

7. Daniel Kadlec, "Annual Reports Reveal New Theme," *USA Today*, March 30, 1994.

8. Brian Dumaine, "The Trouble with Teams," *Fortune*, September 5, 1995.

2

Something Is Not Working: The Implementation Dilemma

We are all faced with a series of great opportunities brilliantly disguised as impossible situations.

—Chuck Swindoll

"Something is not working!" has become an all-too-familiar refrain in many companies faced with the challenge of implementing formalized teams. Companies representing a broad range of industries, with widely differing corporate cultures and circumstances, face similar problems as particular patterns emerge about what is not working. There is in fact a pattern of common dilemmas that arise when companies implement formal teams without fully taking into account the overall corporate culture. This chapter looks at the problems companies generally face, and why.

Patterns of Common Dilemmas

There are three basic patterns seen in companies having difficulty with formal team implementation:

1. Hierarchical patterns
2. Organizational patterns
3. Team patterns

Let's look at each in turn.

Hierarchical Patterns

Symptoms of what's not working come from a number of levels within organizations. For example, senior managers' perspectives typically differ from those of middle management or team leaders, as well as from those of organizational or team members. However, there are some similar occurrences within each hierarchical category.

Senior Managers

Senior managers, typically the ones who initiate the change to formalized teams, logically expect things to be better as a result. They hope for improved productivity, creativity, flexibility, and cost savings, and they believe team spirit can add positive energy and boost morale. However, following implementation, many feel that the organization is not realizing the hoped-for benefits. Some senior managers are unable to point to definite problem signs—customer complaints, being over budget, or being behind on deadlines—yet they feel something is not working. As hard as it might be to believe, many of these senior managers are not aware that what's not working are the teams and teamwork themselves. The managers are often out of the loop or are protected from this information by self-interest or fear of reprisal on the part of the people reporting directly to them.

In other situations, senior managers find themselves dealing with disagreements between or among their direct reports. This might involve individuals trying to protect their own turf, direct reports not being able to come up with a win/win solution, vying for power, or lobbying the boss for support. As you would guess, these behaviors do not reflect optimal team functioning.

Unfortunately, in far too many situations senior managers are not in agreement about why formal teams were implemented or how. They continue to think and behave individually, giving their own messages to whichever part of the organization they manage. Their decision making often reflects their own "silos," which is a myopic view that is focused only on their particular part of the organization. They are typically unable to represent or speak for the whole organization.

Middle Managers

Midlevel managers have their own sets of issues when attempting to adapt to teams. New structures, such as matrix organizations or teams, cause them to feel a loss of control. Some common concerns they voice are "How do I manage these individuals if I don't have any authority over them?" "How do I keep them on track without having direct control over their performance review?" "This decision by consensus stuff takes time; is it worth it?"

Managers who were successful in the past are often upset by the new expectations made of them, and at times they question the need to change. They don't understand what managing differently in the new team environment actually means. How do they change their style without major psychological overhaul? What should they do differently from what they did before? What new awareness and skills are required of them? Why should they be the first to change when no one else—including their boss—is making that effort? These questions, if unanswered, allow these managers to go on as before.

Team Members

Team members and others in the organization find themselves in a similar quandary. They certainly have their own doubts about "this team thing," as they call it, even though many are reveling in it. Typically, many are unsure of what is expected of them in this new operating mode. This is disconcerting to some and comforting to others. For many, not knowing what different behaviors are expected in various team situations creates anxiety and wasted energy in trying to do "the right thing." But it gives other people license to say, "No one told me you expected me to do that." Either way, employees are not asking for clarification. Some remain stuck in the old paradigm of waiting until the boss tells them. Some assume they understand. Others hope it never gets clarified. This creates a situation where new behaviors are based on individuals' assumptions and choices about what is expected.

Another interesting phenomenon is the anger and distrust organization members have of *any* change, including teamwork. They are critical of most changes and ready to point a finger at those who instigated them. This is not surprising in light of the number and type of changes being imposed on organizations today, which inevitably create reactions to teamwork. For example, it seems hypocritical for employees to act together as team members when people must also deal with potential downsizing, fears about job security, or role changes. Survival becomes their primary concern, and the survival mentality leads to behaviors antithetical to teams and teamwork. Some employees keep a low profile and don't "buck the system," speak up, ask questions, or give suggestions. They avoid identifying the real problems that block the implementation of teams. They are just glad to have a job and are not about to overtly put themselves on the line. In turn, they become passive noncontributors to the implementation of teams and can unintentionally sabotage the success of the team concept.

On the other hand, some employees are focused on preserving their jobs by behaving in the other extreme. They try to shine and promote their own individual cause, regardless of its impact on anyone else. Their self-concern and attention to their own success are costly to the team as well.

Although these reactions may be natural in light of the dynamic organizational environment, they are not being acknowledged and managed in today's business world. This is significant since they create obstacles to successful implementation of teams as well as perpetuate skepticism about teams and teamwork.

Organizational Patterns

Unclear or conflicting organizational messages are major issues regarding what's not working in formalizing teams. Senior management teams notoriously are accused of not "walking their talk." They say "Yea team!" and verbally support it, but that's where it ends. They don't seem to model the teamwork they espouse among themselves or with their staff, and they typically go on operating as individuals. Many senior managers often ignore unresolved conflict among themselves while everyone else observes the conflict and feels its impact. Senior managers' lack of total support for formalized teams is reflected in how they communicate and deal with their direct reports.

Senior managers tend to protect their individual turf. This shows up in their vying for or not giving up department resources, or their pushing a technology or decision that benefits individual rather than organizational goals. In turn, their direct reports—whether they be managers, staff members, or team members—similarly tend not to offer win/win, alternative solutions because they feel obliged to protect their boss's and department's control. We see huge duplication of efforts or roles among different functional areas, yet there are few efforts to negotiate and resolve them. This is often due to (1) fear of losing control if negotiations take place, (2) poor communication between silos to even find out about the overlap, or (3) avoidance of conflict in general.

Comical, but quite common, are team or project meetings that become larger than most department meetings. This often results when everyone wants to be part of the meeting "just in case" a decision impacts or threatens their function or area of responsibility. Other team members are not trusted to have "big picture" considerations when they make decisions. Or decision makers send team members who are not empowered to listen and report back. This ensures that the decision maker maintains control, but at the same time it slows down the team decision-making process.

This last scenario is closely linked to the fact that managers or team leaders are still managing in the traditional way. Often, departments are reorganized into teams but are still managed as a hierarchy. A team is formed and the leader, who may or may not be a manager, takes on the characteristics of the autocratic leaders he or she has known so well. Although the team leader may have protested about that style in the past, it's the model he or she knows best. The other extreme is where leaders shy away from the command-and-control style and become reluctant to delegate so as not to "impose" on team members. They would rather take on the responsibility than feel they are being bossy. Neither choice is constructive for optimal teamwork.

A classic conflicting organizational message is about rewards and recognition for teams and teamwork. When rewards are not in sync with expected behaviors, some common thoughts are: "Why bother being successful in teams or teamwork when we are still rewarded as individuals? It's obviously not as important as they say." "There are a few of us pulling the load while others cruise along, and no one notices, cares, or confronts it." There may be nothing positive to reinforce teamwork: no celebrations for team successes; no performance reviews that reflect team and teamwork expectations; and no adjustments in pay, bonuses, or incentives for team performance. There may also be no penalties or repercussions imposed when there is no compliance with or achievement of expected team performance. Without any guidelines or controls to prevent ineffective behavior, formalized teams suffer. And without any recognition or reward to encourage positive examples, formalized teams also suffer.

There is often a lack of understanding and communication about *why* an organization has chosen to formalize and implement some aspect of teams. Organization members hear "We must operate more as a team," "We need improved teamwork," "We need to be more flexible and responsive," and "We need to do more with less." Although these are attempts at explaining "the why," there is no clear and convincing message about the decision, structure, or philosophy adopted for formalizing teams. Coupled with employee cynicism about change, organization members believe this must be the "program du jour": The executive must have read an interesting article about teams, or the organization is just trying to keep up with the latest trends. Engendering support for successful change requires clear and consistent messages about why the organization is formalizing teams and teamwork—messages that are not being delivered.

Another big gap in understanding, communication, and planning relates to what's different today about *how* the company is operating. "What is now expected of me, my manager, team, and department, and in the interaction among all of these? How do we function in a matrix? Whom do I try to please? Whose priorities do I respond to? How do we resolve conflicts? What information do I need to relay, and to whom?" These questions are part of how you operationalize the change toward teams, but the answers are usually not developed or communicated when teams and teamwork are formalized. In situations where a merger or acquisition has occurred, those same concerns relate to how organizational members interact within the two distinct environments and according to whose rules. A smooth, planned transition rarely occurs.

A very common void after implementation of teams is an assessment of how they are doing and if the concept is really working. In other words, is this new way of working achieving the intended results? This type of evaluation is complicated by the fact that expected outcomes have usually not been clearly defined or agreed upon at the outset of the change. In turn, there are no measures to assess progress or results. This makes it difficult to reinforce or celebrate the change. It also thwarts analysis of trends over the long term.

Team Patterns

A distinct subset of what's not working within the broader organizational context is how formalized teams are actually functioning. Unclear goals or lack of agreement about the goals is common. Team members often do not understand each other's background and expertise in general or what contributions they can make toward achieving the team's goal beyond their traditional role. In turn, team members' talents are often underutilized. This can create an atmosphere of apathy or annoyance. Team members frequently react by saying, "That's typical; let them fend for themselves!" and choose not to offer valuable information or expertise.

As described earlier, traditional leadership and employee style issues abound. Both affect how teams function. Some team members expect and like the traditional autocratic leadership style, while others resent and fight it. Many team members are "doing their own thing" and operating in silos to accomplish their part of the project, with only an occasional check-in or meeting. Many still feel that team meetings are a waste and that it is better to work individually, communicating only through e-mail or memo.

Some may not be pulling their weight, while others over-compensate and take on too much. Individuals are often not held accountable for what they do or don't contribute to the team. Most struggle to grasp the concept that all team members should share responsibility for the team's success. Traditional employee and manager mind-sets about individual contributors discourage shared responsibility and self-regulation for team success. Accountability becomes a serious issue.

Resolving conflicts, managing differences, and coming to consensus are major challenges facing most teams. They reflect the struggle in making the transition from past organizational norms and accepted behaviors to the new paradigms necessary for formalized teams to function at their best.

Implementation Myths

Numerous myths, still alive and well, often result in strategies that hinder organizations' successful implementation of formal teams.

Myths About Teamwork

The first myth relates to teamwork. There is a strong belief that it should occur naturally. After all, everyone has worked in teams before, so teamwork is easy and not any big deal to do! The myth continues with the notion that we are all professionals, intelligent people, some even with advanced degrees—we should be able to figure this out!

If teamwork doesn't work immediately, the next myth rationalizes that time will make it happen: "If we just keep working at it long enough and hard enough, it should work." And if it doesn't, the myth about personality conflicts as the biggest obstacle to teamwork rears its ugly head. In other words, "If it weren't for Bob and Jane, this would be a high-performing team!" Then there is the myth about going off on a fun retreat: "Let's have a few laughs, climb some mountains and then we'll come back a high-performing team."

Now, don't get us wrong. There is some truth to these myths, but none individually will ensure a high-performing team. For example, time does help a team gel and get to know each other; laughing and having fun together builds rapport. Personality conflicts do drain a team. Intelligent people can intellectually understand team concepts. However, functioning as a high-performance team requires new and different skills, techniques, and styles along with new organizational norms. The myths detract from dealing with the real issues.

Myths About Change

Another myth is that a high-performing team can survive and thrive in spite of an organizational environment which has not been changed to support teamwork. Although this can happen, over the long term the team loses its incentive from the hierarchical and organizational pressures described earlier in this chapter.

The myth that there is no need to plan the change toward formalizing teams is quite pervasive. The belief is that you just do it. You declare teamwork as part of your vision, you deem your department to be a team, you cheerlead your newly merged organization to pull together and be a team. You restructure, and then all else follows. No need for dramatic fanfare or extensive planning. We can all figure it out and do what we must.

If only it worked that way.

This change myth is linked to many managers' belief that if they espouse teamwork, it will happen, whether or not their own behaviors are consistent. Or managers think that if they say it and then behave it, others will surely get the message and follow. There is no need to reinforce or hold folks accountable—everybody should know to do it! The hope is that others will eventually get it. Won't they? You would be astonished at how many senior managers are neither aware of the need for nor are comfortable with holding others accountable for the "softer" and more esoteric "stuff" such as teamwork.

Typical Implementation Strategies

Many of these myths directly relate to some typical strategies employed when formalizing teams. A classic one is to make the change and announce it: "We are now a matrix organization," "We will now have interdisciplinary teams," "We must work together as an organizational team," etc. Leaders talk it up every chance they get, but what is often missing are the details: why we're doing this, what's expected, and how it will occur. An announcement and enthusiasm cannot stand on their own. A plan of action must be put in place.

A second common strategy is to train everyone to death. The belief that added skills will ensure the success of a new concept is only partially true. The training typically focuses on knowledge and skill in how to be a team but does not address the organizational issues described earlier in this chapter, such as senior management buy-in and agreement, inconsistent styles, inconsistent reward systems, or unclear definition of the new team direction. Such oversights fuel questions or hostilities from training participants and often derail the benefits of the training or the skills learned. This typically happens when training is one of the first events, or many times the only event, to occur when formalizing teams. Attending to the organizational and corporate culture issues is typically ignored while training takes precedence.

Not considering the current corporate culture is by far one of the most common oversights and serious deterrents to successful change toward teams. This includes ensuring senior management agreement and consistency on why, what, and how the change should occur. It involves administering to the corporate culture to ensure there are no cloudy, inconsistent, or conflicting messages going on about the individual versus the team, what is said versus done, traditional versus new managerial style requirements, what is rewarded, etc. It means attending to any current management policies and practices that may be out of sync with a team-oriented environment. It means dealing with an employee "survival mentality" that may be working against actualizing team goals.

Other strategies employed by organizations have focused on creating opportunities for teamwork. This is done through identifying issues or challenges to be addressed by a team, creating or declaring new teams across traditional boundaries and hierarchies and beyond internal boundaries, and designing new structures. Again, subsequent steps are usually missing.

The most common strategy has been to train managers and employees on teamwork. The most consistent and glaring void has been the lack of attention to corporate culture and the planning of a change strategy to create a supportive culture for their formalized team concept.

3

Corporate Culture: The Missing Link

You can have change without improvement, but you cannot have improvement without change.

—A Wise Old Friend

The point is clear with regard to revitalizing our organizations through the use of formal teams. You cannot succeed in your attempt to formalize teams unless you attach the critical missing link—corporate culture—to the change effort.

This chapter examines corporate culture in general and why it is typically overlooked, what corporate cultures and subcultures are, who creates them and can change them, and the various aspects of a culture that support or hinder team success.

Surrounded by Culture

Whether you are aware of it or not, culture is all around you. Every time you travel to a different country, state, city, or town, you may be struck by how unique places can be in their customs, pace, or behavioral patterns (subtle or obvious). Have you ever noticed, even in airports, how the atmosphere in places like New York, Los Angeles, Pocatello, or Tokyo reflects the different overall cultures of the region?

Corporations have distinct cultures as well. Walk into various organizations and "feel" the environment—for example, how people greet or even look at you, if they do at all. What people say or don't say, the furniture, the bulletin boards, and the nonverbal cues can all be very telling. While walking through the halls of one major pharmaceutical company, we couldn't help but feel people's detachment from their coworkers and visitors, as compared with the warmth and connectedness exhibited by workers in another pharmaceutical company. It is the same industry and same region of the country, but there are totally different environments. Even within the "warm" pharmaceutical company, the Michigan division has a very "Midwest" environment, as compared with the northeast or Belgian divisions. On top of regional differences, there are different cultural styles among, say, salespeople, accountants, chemists, or engineers.

Culture affects many aspects of our personal and professional life. Consider this definition of culture, from the *American Heritage Dictionary:* "the arts, beliefs, customs, institutions, and all other products of human work and thought created by a people or group of people at a particular time." This is such a broad definition, so far-reaching, that you can almost think about a hierarchy of cultures, with the most macro perspective being civilization (compare Eastern and Western cultures). Next are countries, with their own national cultures, which are in turn broken down into provinces, regions, states, and cities or towns, where there are distinctive ways of acting and being. Overlay religious, racial, and ethnic backgrounds, and you have additional subcultures.

In the corporate world there is a similar hierarchy of cultural possibilities that provide additional overlays. A multinational corporate office, for example, has numerous divisions and departments in locations all over the world. It has service or product business units, each with its own cultural flare, in addition to the overall common corporate culture. Economic, political, and environmental forces also influence the various levels of culture described. Then, of course, each industry and specialization adds another layer to this cultural hierarchy.

Why Is Culture Overlooked?

We often overlook culture, for a number of reasons. First, we tend not to think about our cultures, whether they be personal or organizational, as they are so deeply rooted. The patterns of beliefs, values, and behaviors are so internalized that the cultural rituals become automatic and unconscious. Second, the component parts of a culture are hard to grab hold of. Ask people to describe their cultural background or company culture and you will get diverse responses even from those within the same culture, as people select different dimensions that are important to them.

Third, we tend to notice culture acutely only when confronted by changes from or differences in what we're used to. In fact, we expect others to have customs and cultures similar to our own and are surprised and annoyed when they don't. For example, if you move to a small town after living in New York City, you may be uncomfortable with the relative lack of anonymity or slower pace of life. Our reactions to the differences usually signal our awareness: "That's strange." "Why did they do that?" "How could they even think that?" "What do they mean by that?" "They are so slow!"

If you work in one organization for any length of time and then move to another, or if your company undergoes a merger, your sensitivities are heightened about the distinctions. Things previously taken for granted become acutely noticed. The comparisons can create stress or relief, depending on your comfort zone.

A fourth reason why culture is overlooked is that, considering its anthropological roots, most people see it as a given and unchangeable. People tend to see organizational culture as similarly unmalleable.

The result of all this is that culture remains overlooked, whether we are interacting with others personally, attempting to transfer technology within a company or to different countries, creating business alliances, merging companies, or making major organizational changes. A profound example of ignoring cultural differences was when American companies assumed that the Japanese would adjust to our cars' left-sided steering wheels, or to our large-sized refrigerators—which could hardly fit into many Japanese apartments. Similarly, a company on the verge of merging with or acquiring another company rarely assesses whether the target company's culture is compatible with its own, or makes a proactive effort to consciously merge the two distinct cultures and create a new one.

Formalizing teams is another important example of culture not being dealt with. Although installing formalized teams into a culture may create a heightened awareness of the existing culture, it often does not stimulate action in addressing the culture. Instead, corporate culture remains the missing link in successful change efforts around teams.

Defining Corporate Culture

We need to define corporate culture before we can describe how to revamp it. An executive once jokingly described it as like "a fungus in the air-conditioning: It's hard to put your hands around it, but it's everywhere!"

Corporate culture generally refers to the environment or personality of an organization, with all its multifaceted dimensions. It is "the way we do things around here," with an aura of its own, much like an individual's personality. More specifically, we divide corporate culture into four aspects, as illustrated in Exhibit 3-1.

Ritualized Patterns

Culture comprises the ritualized patterns of beliefs, values, and behaviors shared by organization members. These rituals and traditions may relate to political, economic, or social mores and may be built around such things as relationships with customers and coworkers, status, work ethics, openness, individuality versus collectivism, and how work gets done. For example, status or political traditions can be shown by the hierarchy of degrees and pedigrees in a clinical, medical, or research environment, or in the rift between factory workers and salespeople in a manu-

Exhibit 3-1. A definition of corporate culture.

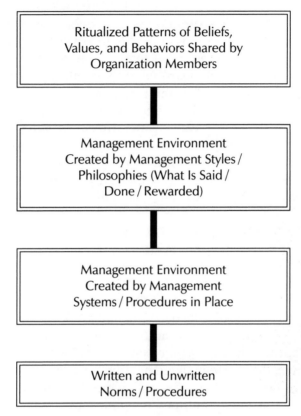

Ritualized Patterns of Beliefs, Values, and Behaviors Shared by Organization Members

Management Environment Created by Management Styles / Philosophies (What Is Said / Done / Rewarded)

Management Environment Created by Management Systems / Procedures in Place

Written and Unwritten Norms / Procedures

facturing environment. The action-oriented, "ready, fire, aim" pattern of decision making prevalent in one culture can be contrasted with the "analysis paralysis" pattern of another.

Then there is food and dress. Attorneys' Title Insurance Fund of Orlando, Florida, takes tremendous pride in the abundant display of food that is an essential element of every meeting and get-together, symbolizing caring and the social and fun aspect of working together. M&M/Mars takes such pride in its products that the company's snacks are part of every morning, afternoon, and evening meeting. Compare these two examples to organizations where employees are not even allowed to have food or drink in their conference rooms or at their desks. As for dress, IBM's classic white shirt and tie of the past has given way to a casual, more relaxed look. Yet even "casual" can mean different things to different organizations: jeans and T-shirts in one office, neat and pressed trousers and shirts with ties in another.

Many rituals are so ingrained that organization members may not always be conscious of or able to articulate them. A new employee, faced with pressure to conform, is likely to notice these patterns or quickly learn what they are by trial and error. The newcomer might learn the rituals by receiving such messages as "We call everyone around here by his or her first name," "Meetings typically start fifteen minutes late," "I wouldn't question their judgment if I were you," "Remember, the doctor has the final word," or "The customer is always right." Such statements convey important information on the environment and what is or is not acceptable.

Management Styles and Philosophies

Culture is also the environment created by pervasive management styles, philosophies, and behaviors. It relates to communication, decision making, motivation, coaching, innovation, planning, problem solving, accountability, and other aspects of leadership. Is it a command-and-control, hierarchical environment, or one that is more participative? What are the underlying philosophies that drive management behavior?

When Leonard Roberts was named president of Radio Shack, he immediately outlined his philosophy, which specified only two roles that organization members can play: One is to serve the customer, the other is to serve someone who does.[1] This was a portent of what he was going to instill and expect of others regarding teamwork. Alex Trotman, the CEO at Ford, challenges his staff to argue with him, give him off-the-wall ideas, and find weak spots in his thinking.

The style that surfaces as the most powerful influence on the culture is what is espoused, practiced, and rewarded. When those are consistent, leaders create a consistent message about the prevalent style and environment. When they are not, there are conflicting messages. For instance, advocating teamwork but not holding others accountable for team-oriented behaviors is seen as lip service. If a leader talks team but acts autocratically, the latter is seen as the prevalent style. If the leader rewards behaviors contrary to teamwork, those behaviors will be the ones modeled, regardless of the leader's team-oriented style.

Management Systems and Procedures

Another important aspect of corporate culture is the management environment created by the systems, procedures, and policies in place within the organization. They may be clearly stated and written, but they may also be assumed from what is *not* in place. The systems, procedures, and policies convey the concerns and priorities of a company. What is your organization structure? Who and what is celebrated and how often? What is measured and rewarded? What type of people are hired, and how do they learn about the organization, its priorities, and what is expected of them as new employees? How are people developed for their current or future roles, and is there an expectation about that? What types of policies exist around work/ family issues such as telecommuting, flextime, and child care, and how flexible are the policies?

Some of the more subtle yet equally important systems that create powerful messages include the physical structure, layout, and decor of the office space and reception areas. Are there higher-status offices in terms of size, floor number, or windows? Is there an open-space environment? What are the waiting rooms like? Who are the "guards"? Do visitors feel like criminals, are they made to feel unimportant or unnoticed, or are they welcomed and made to feel at home? The organization also communicates about itself via the image it expresses to the public, through ads (part of the selections procedure that also says much about the company and the kind of employee sought) or annual reports (a communications device that shows how the company portrays itself to the public).

Written and Unwritten Norms and Procedures

The culture is created as much by unwritten norms and procedures as it is by the written ones. There are often assumed and expected behaviors but no written policies stating them. For example, in many organizations people work late or don't leave until after the boss does, whereas in other places you can't find anyone around after 4:00 P.M. Socializing may be expected in one environment but not in another. An executive may leave his or her door open, but employees may not be comfortable walking in if the executive's actions are contrary to the open-door policy. Whether the systems are written or assumed, or inferred from not being in place, they contribute to the defined culture.

Many organizations are unaware of the various components of their culture or the powerful messages created by management styles, philosophies, systems, and policies whether in place or not. Even more so, organizations seem to be unaware of the conflicting messages and obstacles they create when installing a major change initiative such as formalized teams.

What Is a Subculture?

Earlier in this chapter we spoke of culture as a hierarchy. When we speak of the corporate culture, we refer to the overall organizational entity. The subculture is a subset or component part of the larger organization, with its own set of rituals, management styles, systems, and procedures that may be written or assumed. Each succeeding level on an organization chart—each different division, department, section, work unit, and location—has its own subculture.

Functional areas within a culture also have their own subculture. Compare the environments in research and development, marketing and sales, and manufacturing, and you find marked differences. Put people from various staff functions such as human resources, finance, and legal in the same room and you can hear the differences in vocabulary, objectives, and styles.

Different industries such as government, health care, high tech, and oil all have their own overarching cultures as well as distinct organization subcultures. The uniformed U.S. military has an overarching culture, with four distinct subcultures in the Air Force, Army, Navy, and Marine Corps. If you dissect those subcultures further, you find what could be called sub-subcultures; in the Air Force there are the flying unit and ground-based unit. The health care industry has traditionally had an overarching culture, and each related subindustry, such as hospitals, long-term care facilities, and home health agencies, similarly has unique cultural and subcultural differences. Then, of course, within each individual facility there would be distinctive cultures and subcultures.

Subcultures are strongly influenced by the overall organizational culture and are in some instances governed by many of the umbrella philosophies, structures, and policies. However, an organization's subcultures are never identical to each other or to the overall culture. Each has its distinctions.

Who Creates the Culture or Subculture?

The most senior leadership of the overall organizational entity creates the corporate culture. Depending on the structure of an organization, this might be a chairperson, CEO, president, or executive team. The most senior leadership of the subsets within the larger organization creates the subculture. This could be one manager or a group of managers: a division president, general manager, vice-president, department manager, or management team.

In a newly merged or acquired organization, usually the senior leadership of the prearranged "parent" or the more economically powerful entity creates or maintains the culture. A business alliance or partnership between two or more entities would require the senior leadership team of all the entities to create a new overall culture; if not, they would maintain their individual cultures—which unfortunately is typically the case.

A company may overlay a temporary structure onto an existing one, such as an interdepartmental committee to accomplish a particular objective across organizational lines. We call this a collateral organization (see Chapter 9). In that case, the new team itself could create a temporary subculture across departments to accomplish the objective.

Changing the Culture

Despite its ingrained nature, a corporate culture (or subculture) can be changed. This is not always easy, since it can mean forcing people to confront issues, other workers, and differences—something most of us choose to avoid. Yet changing a culture can reveal tremendous, usually untapped, opportunities.

New senior executives can produce dramatic shifts. Arthur C. Martinez, who recently became chief executive at Sears, Roebuck, is attempting a virtual cultural revolution at the giant retailer, in part to decentralize and restructure Sears, in part to stress customer service, and in part to change how people feel about and do their jobs. Efforts involve pep rallies, training sessions, discussion groups, and new operating structures, job descriptions, evaluation policies, and compensation systems.[2]

When an overall corporate culture changes, as at Sears, it clearly affects the subcultures within it. Yet the subcultures will still have their own personalities within the new, larger framework.

Even more importantly, a subculture can change in spite of or apart from the broader culture. There is much more flexibility and freedom to effect change within a subculture than is commonly realized or acted upon. And just as distinct subcultures have evolved within the parameters of an overall culture, they can continue to evolve and change without disturbing the broader culture. This creates many possibilities and opportunities for culture change to ensure successful teams.

Just who can change the culture or subculture? Although the traditional formula is to link the possibility of change to the most senior executive, given the existence of subcultures, someone much lower down—such as a department manager—can also be the source of important change.

Examples of Cultural Variety

The variety of cultures created by leaders is fascinating. U.S. President Lyndon Johnson created the Great Society; GE's Jack Welch, Disney's Michael Eisner, and IBM's Lou Gerstner have made their distinctive marks and created powerful and unique corporate cultures.

Some noteworthy cultures offer us a look at rituals, values, management philosophies, and policies at work:

Saturn, the auto manufacturer, prides itself on its democratic and open culture. There are no time clocks or reserved parking spaces, and there is a strong concept of leading in partnership. For example, in each plant, an employee representing the United Auto Workers shares managing and decision making with the Saturn manager. Suppliers and retailers interact right on the factory floor in partnership. Employees are open about what goes on and have a continuous stream of visitors coming through the factory.

Wabash National, which customizes truck trailers, has a more hierarchical and somewhat paternal environment. Chairman Donald J. Ehrlich is a proponent of efficiency and teams. Wabash has a fast-paced environment where productivity reigns and hard work is rewarded. Penalties are imposed for being one minute late, and communication is encouraged as long as it doesn't take too much time.[3]

The athletic shoe company *Nike* has a cultlike corporate loyalty. There is an elite group within the company called EKINs (Nike spelled backward), who are the direct frontline liaisons with retailers. EKINs have their own subculture within Nike, even sporting tattoos of the company logo. Reebok, in contrast, has a more individualistic culture, with more balance between work and personal life. However, even Reebok has an est-like subculture lurking within as a result of chief executive Paul Fireman's interest in est (the human potential program founded by Werner Erhard in the 1970s).[4]

The editorial division of the *Fort Lauderdale Sun-Sentinel*, one of the more profitable newspapers within the Chicago Tribune Company, exudes a fast-paced, action-packed environment—understandable when you think about their deadline to produce a product every single day. Added to that is the creative spirit of journalists, artists, photographers, copy editors, and the like, who each create their own distinct subculture and reputation. The large glass-encased office of the vice-president/editor smack in the middle of the newsroom adds just a little more edge to the atmosphere, as do the different personalities of the last two individuals who have had that position.

There are an infinite variety of distinct cultures and subcultures; this small sample illustrates only some of the rituals, values, management philosophies, and policies that can influence a culture. And an added number of highly complex cultures are taking form as the growing number of acquisitions and mergers leads to new, blended cultures.

Having a Supportive Culture for Teams

Culture is a powerful force. It must be considered when instigating a change, because it affects how the organization receives and fosters that change. The ultimate success of a change toward formalized teams is contingent upon the culture being supportive. If teams are to be an integrated aspect of how work gets done, they must become an integrated aspect of the culture.

Currently, formalized teams are usually overlaid onto the culture—typically introduced and added onto the existing culture, instead of integrated into it. The culture is neither examined as to its fit nor altered. As you might imagine, if they are not addressed, the values, beliefs, rituals, management styles, systems, and policies in place within the culture work against this team overlay.

If the culture does not support teams, obstacles continue to appear and eventually derail team success. Organization members continue to go to team training, only to return to and complain about the nonsupportive culture. The organization continues to grow frustrated with the lack of results and rationalizes that "teams don't seem to work around here."

In the past, this lack of attention to the culture or to a strategy for creating a supportive culture worked. This was because teams typically were temporary, ad hoc, and informal, operating within the existing structures and hierarchy. When all was said and done, teams were seen as just a nicety, an adjunct to how work got done. For example, two or more managers might have seen a need to collaborate on problem solving or tap one another's resources. They would do so through a temporary team and then revert back to the hierarchy. There was no need to create an ongoing supportive infrastructure and culture for formal teams. A quality team was another example where time sort of stood still for a few hours while team members focused on team-work, until they went back to the traditional hierarchical way of operating within their departments.

Today, however, organizations have sanctioned and formal-ized teams as a critical way of accomplishing work. They have restructured the organization and installed formalized proce-dures or processes for new ways to work. Yet these dramatic changes are still being treated as minor, natural occurrences that neither interact with nor are impacted by the organization's cul-ture, powerful as it is. The changes are just being overlaid onto the culture. This is a tremendous mistake. All of these adjust-ments require cultures that support and nurture them and the inherently new way of doing work.

An additional problem is faced by companies involved in mergers, acquisitions, and alliances where the expectation is that all parties will become a new "organization team." But the cul-tural differences—and, in some instances, conflicts—are not dealt with. The newly merged organization is merely overlaid onto the two original cultures. Combining distinct cultures re-quires attention and support, if the organization team and newly merged functions are to operate at their best.

Examples of Cultures That Support or Hinder Teams

You cannot draw conclusions from the surface or overall "feel" of a culture as to whether that culture is or is not supportive of teams. This requires more in-depth analysis of the various as-pects of the culture: its values, rituals, management philoso-phies, styles, and policies. A culture that engenders tremendous corporate spirit and loyalty does not necessarily support teams and teamwork. Take the example of the old IBM, before its new emphasis on teamwork. The old IBM valued individual contrib-utors above all, so highly that the behavior of the so-called wild ducks was vastly preferred.

Then there is the motorcycle manufacturer Harley-David-son, which has an interesting and dichotomous culture of individualism *and* collectivism. The people there have a tremen-dously strong spirit and almost cultlike feeling of being part of the only American motorcycle manufacturing company. Seventy to 80 percent of the employees ride motorcycles and value the individualism that is reflective of their eagle symbol and Easy Rider image. They refuse to call themselves "teams," even when working as such. Instead, workers refer to themselves as committees or work groups, for fear of losing their individuality to teams. Yet this culture is not unsupportive of teams.

All cultures can have select aspects that may or may not support teams: It is not an all-or-nothing thing. At Harley-Davidson, a flat structure with only five levels between hourly workers and the CEO is a supportive aspect of the culture. Management emphasizes how people do things, not just the results achieved. Management's solution to employees' negative reactions to the word *team* is to encourage teams as short-term, as needed options within a large bag of tools. Managers know that work groups and committees thrive, so why insist on using an emotionally triggered word? On the other hand, the company still struggles with some traditional management practices that prevail within the environment, such as controlled, autocratic decision-making styles, and it continues to reward that behavior, which works against the collective spirit.

Clean Cut In, an Austin-based landscape design, construction, and maintenance company, wanted to create a culture of teamwork that motivated long-standing, skilled employees to help new workers understand the culture, policies, etc. The company devised a system that recorded when long-standing employees did so. If newcomers eventually became partners in the company, those who had helped them along their path were rewarded with a bonus matching up to 10 percent of the partners' profit sharing.[5] That's an interesting example of a policy that supports the desired team-oriented behavior.

Levi Strauss bases one-third of an employee's evaluation on "aspirational behavior" as depicted in its corporate aspiration statements. Aspects include recognition of individuals and teams contributing to the company's success, empowerment of employees, and management's showing commitment to supporting the success of others.[6] Regarding its team culture, Levi

Strauss has developed a philosophy, key values, and expected behaviors, and it holds individuals accountable for them.

Miller Breweries is an example of a company culture where teamwork was being encouraged and rewarded through competition but ultimately worked against overall company success. Individual breweries competed with each other to be the lowest-cost producer. This created tremendous team spirit and effort *within* each brewery. However, the survival-of-the-fittest message fostered winners and losers and pushed competition among breweries. This led to hoarding of important information, technology, and success secrets that would have benefited all the breweries. The company is now rethinking this philosophy and reward system.

Saturn created an organization structure to support a team-oriented environment. So-called decision rings articulate how people are represented at different organization levels and where those levels interact and overlap, and how action councils ensure involvement at all levels. Work units are self-managed and responsible for approximately thirty functions including work planning, job assignments, training, and self-corrective action. There are operating norms and decision checklists to assist workers in such things as tapping expertise, owning responsibilities, and achieving consensus. Clearly these are aspects of Saturn's culture that support teams.

However, there are still aspects of the Saturn culture that hinder complete actualization of this team culture. One is rooted in how management deals with poor performance. If a work team does not or cannot execute certain functions and responsibilities, management has been known to remove that particular responsibility and reabsorb it. Management removes the responsibility not only from the one team having trouble, but from all of the teams as well. This behavior is inconsistent with the other, better reinforced messages about self-responsibility and empowerment. It represents more of a traditional management mind-set of "Well, if you can't deal with this, we'll just have to," rather than a coaching mode to foster accountability.

Another aspect of the Saturn culture working against teams is that management still focuses and follows up on the *what* versus the *how*, or people aspect, of teaming. In turn, the measurement-and-reward system focuses on quality, adherence to schedules, and meeting training objectives without attention to measuring or rewarding teamwork. Now that the organization has discovered it is not fully realizing its team-oriented culture, this aspect of the environment is being investigated.

And take the reputed style of *Jim Manzi*, ex-CEO of *Lotus*, as an example of how management style can potentially undermine teamwork. If rumors are true of Manzi having fired fifty-five executives within ten years, and not very gracefully,[7] imagine how that might affect the behavior of the surviving executives. One could argue that firing is not a bad thing to do if people are not meeting performance standards or are not compatible with the culture. However, the effect on the culture is markedly different from the intent. The organization members typically tremble in fear. Candor, risk taking, and cooperation go out the door, and instead there is a culture of keeping a low profile and being self-protective. Management style, unwittingly or not, sends powerful messages to the organization and influences the culture.

These examples show the various aspects of an organization's culture that can support or hinder a successful team culture. If organizations are to be successful in supporting teams, there needs to be consistency in support and a reduction of obstacles.

This consistency does not mean that all cultures must be the same. We are not advocating a one-size-fits-all approach. Rather, we are reinforcing the need for an assessment of the conscious or unconscious beliefs, patterns of behavior, management styles, and policies that support or hinder teams, and the need for an enlightened and conscious decision to make such adjustments.

Notes

1. Laura E. Keeton, "Radio Shack's President Adds Some Spark to Its Image," *The Wall Street Journal*, July 31, 1995.

2. Judith H. Dobrzynski, "Yes, He's Revived Sears. But Can He Reinvent It?" *The New York Times*, January 7, 1996.

3. Robert L. Rose, "Hard Driving—A Productivity Push at Wabash National Puts Firm on a Roll," *The Wall Street Journal*, September 7, 1995.

4. Kenneth Labich, "Nike vs. Reebok—A Battle for Hearts, Minds & Feet," *Fortune*, September 18, 1995.

5. "Co-Owners Devise Unique Reward System," Update, *HRM Magazine*, October 1995.

6. Russell Mitchell, "Managing By Values—Is Levi Strauss' Approach Visionary or Flaky?" *Business Week*, August 1, 1994.

7. "After 99 Days, Jim Manzi Leaves IBM," *The Wall Street Journal*, October 12, 1995.

4

Changing Culture to Support Teams

There is nothing more difficult to take in hand, more peril-
ous to conduct, or more uncertain in its success than to take
the lead in the introduction of a new order of things.

—Niccolò Machiavelli, *The Prince*

The critical first step in successfully installing and supporting
teams is appreciating the magnitude and importance of the
change required in most cultures. Underestimating the power of
corporate culture or, conversely, being overwhelmed by the
sheer complexity of it can jeopardize your attempts at successful
change.

Chapter 3 explained how to recognize corporate culture and
begin to get a handle on the various aspects of a culture that
might require adjustment to support teams. The values, patterns
of behaviors, management styles, and infrastructures in place
are all possible targets for change. But it's also important to recognize how to go about effecting change, something most managers don't really understand, as reflected by many of the
change myths described in earlier chapters.

Larry Bossidy, CEO of Allied Signal, once delivered a key-
note address at a human resources conference in which he discussed teamwork and the importance of moving to a more
horizontal organization. When asked how he was going about

it, he replied that the company was just at the beginning stages and was open to any ideas.

Tom Peters once spoke to a company on customer service and cited his research examples of different strategies companies have employed to achieve excellent customer service. However, when asked how to change a company's culture, he was unable to articulate a clear, step-by-step process on the key requirements for doing so.

This chapter focuses on some of the requirements for approaching a culture change, as a prelude to the step-by-step process and the model for change that is introduced in Chapter 5. Although many of the requirements sound logical, you may be surprised how organizations don't use logic when approaching culture change in support of teams, new structures, or mergers.

The Current Corporate State

We surveyed one hundred diversified corporate and health care organizations to learn about how corporations today are dealing with culture change. As a baseline, we asked how many had recently participated in one or more organizational changes, such as being part of a merger or acquisition, forming an alliance, or increasing the utilization of teams; all of these circumstances require attention to creating, merging, or changing a corporate culture to support a team-oriented environment. The results are shown in Exhibit 4-1. Out of one hundred organiza-

Exhibit 4-1. Breakdown (in percent) of recent organizational changes in one hundred corporations surveyed.

▸ A merger	15%
▸ An acquisition	22
▸ Forming an alliance	41
▸ Increasing the utilization of teams	78
▸ None of the above	5

Note: Figures do not add up to 100 percent because many organizations had more than one change effort going on.

tions, 95 percent had recently experienced one or more of those changes, with 78 percent increasing the utilization of teams, 41 percent forming alliances, and 37 percent involved in acquisitions or mergers. There is a clear message in the data about the need for effective teams and teamwork in these situations. However, the need for addressing the culture and the know-how to do so are not as clear, as shown in Exhibit 4-2.

Although 51 percent of respondents felt that their organization understood the need to address culture issues, only 31 percent felt that their organization had the knowledge, skills, and ability to address those issues. This was reinforced further by

Exhibit 4-2. Breakdown (in percent) on the know-how to address the culture in one hundred corporations surveyed.

Questions	Percent in Agreement
1. My organization understands the need to address organization culture issues with regard to mergers, acquisitions, alliances, and/or supporting the use of teams.	51%
2. My organization has the knowledge, skills, and ability to address organization culture issues to ensure successful mergers, acquisitions, alliances, and/or utilization of teams.	31
3. Our organization has a plan to manage the culture change associated with our merger, acquisition, alliance, or teams.	39
4. Our organization has assessed its current culture and identified changes needed to support the new culture created by a merger, acquisition, alliance, or teams.	36
5. Our senior managers have a clear and agreed-upon goal for the culture change.	31
6. Our senior managers have clearly identified the results expected from the culture change.	31
7. Our organization has examined and altered its personnel and administrative systems to support the new culture.	24
8. Training is an important part of our plan.	56

the lack of strategies employed in addressing the culture. Only 39 percent had a plan to manage the culture change and only 36 percent had assessed their current culture and identified the changes needed to support the new culture. Thirty-one percent felt that senior managers had a clear and agreed-upon goal for the culture change and had identified the results expected from it. Only 24 percent of the organizations had examined and altered their infrastructures to support the new team culture, but training was seen as a primary aspect of their change plans by 56 percent. This is not surprising, since training is a commonly relied-on solution to cultural change. These findings reinforce the need for a framework on how to create a new culture or change one to support the formalized concept of teams.

How Organizations Approach Culture Change

Most organizations do not approach culture change systematically and comprehensively. Instead, they tend to assume change will occur on its own, or they undertake only piecemeal efforts, or they fail to change the overlying environment.

Assuming Change Will Occur

A common assumption is that the cultural issues will resolve themselves, given the merit and reasons for the change. Such assumptions are often mistaken. When negotiations were thwarted during the proposed merger of Wachovia and Suntrust, the biggest issues were over who would run the company. Yet the feeling was that it would be "worked out" because of the incentives to merge.[1] In another case, although it was generally known that Price Club and Costco had very different cultures, their incentives to merge were strong. But there was no in-depth analysis of how distinct the two cultures were on the front end, and no effort to merge the cultures thereafter. They broke up after one year.[2] These are examples of how the cultural issues were not addressed, based on assumptions that they really didn't need to be.

Undertaking Piecemeal Efforts

When it is attempted, creating, merging, or changing cultures is often tried through various, somewhat piecemeal, methods. It is not worked through in a planned, step-by-step process. The particular actions that senior management sees as important are the ones initiated, but such limited steps are clearly not sufficient to support overall and lasting change. Each of the following examples shows important aspects of changing a culture, but each is also missing important elements.

Deutsche Telekom, Europe's largest telecommunications company, needed to change its culture to deal with a deregulated environment. CEO Ron Sommer set new performance criteria and told folks to be prepared to meet them or step aside.[3] But stating new expectations and holding people accountable is only one element of a change strategy.

In another example, *IBM Q&IT* (Quality and Information Technology, an organization within IBM's North American Sales and Services) was trying to create a more team-oriented environment after it restructured into a matrix. The initial thought was simply to provide team training for all teams. With some consultation and assistance, Q&IT's management were convinced to approach it as a culture change necessitating a broader process.

A major utility company similarly needed to turn around its culture to flourish in a more deregulated environment. It needed to become more decentralized and team-oriented and to tackle the slow decision-making process, upward delegation, and analysis-paralysis syndrome that were pervasive in a regulated environment (which was really a way for people to avoid being wrong). The company's strategy was to conduct an analysis of the current culture against what their future culture should be, and then to design and conduct a mandatory training program around that. Needless to say, the culture change was not realized. The company's next action was to conduct another program on decision-making skills, hoping it would stimulate change. Yet a key ingredient still missing was to have senior management actively approach this as a culture change and examine its own styles, systems, and procedures that were getting in the way of the change.

George Fisher, CEO of *Kodak,* set out to change the company culture to become less hierarchical, make decisions faster, take more risks, and increase accountability and spirit. His strategies included actively pushing decisions downward, being accessible and approachable, creating a coaching environment, and linking pay to performance.[4] But again, other important elements were missing in order to ensure that those changes were modeled throughout the organization.

Not Changing the Environment

People become what their environment is and act in ways their environment reinforces. Change cannot occur and endure if the environment does not support that change.

We learned this lesson some years ago when we worked at the Harvard School of Dental Medicine. The school was attempting to train medical and dental students to work in teams, but it overlooked the fact that the environment was antithetical to teams. The school was run as a traditional hierarchical environment, with the professors modeling an autocratic style in their interactions with students. Moreover, at the time the medical and dental professions were far from espousing a team-oriented philosophy. Yet the students were expected to become team players, acting as team leaders of diversified specialists and facilitating teamwork. We watched student after student become angry about how non-team-oriented their treatment was and about how the school was run. We sincerely believed the students were ripe for change and would have behaved differently if they had been taught how. After one month of a very intensive training program that included team clinical practice, changes in student behavior did occur. However, soon after, they went back into "the system" and many forgot what they'd learned about teams, acting instead in the ways of and becoming part of the very thing they hated.

This is just a small sample of the different thoughts and efforts that occur in organizations trying to create change. If they could pull together all of the pieces and add a few more, a more targeted plan would be in place. Many of the pieces are there, yet companies fall short of a strategic process for planning the change. Without a realistic plan, regardless of the power and track record of the senior managers, the best of intentions are not enough to achieve the expected results of the change.

Requirements for Approaching a Culture Change Toward Teams

The following requirements, shown in Exhibit 4-3, need to be considered when you think about and approach a culture change to support teams and teamwork. They provide a framework for understanding the challenges when embarking on such an effort. The step-by-step process described in Chapter 5 can then be used to achieve the desired outcome.

Conscious Decisions

The first step toward change begins with the decision of the most senior manager or managers of an overall company culture or particular subculture to address that culture. Coca-Cola's Roberto Goizueta, Kodak's George Fisher, or IBM's Lou Gerstner are examples of CEOs making conscious decisions to effect change in their overall culture.

The general manager of the Latin American office of Rohm & Haas, the director of Bristol-Myers Squibb's Biostatistics and Data Management Department, and the vice-president of AMI Semiconductors' sales division are managers who made decisions to effect change in their subcultures to support their team concepts.

In the arena of mergers and acquisitions, an example can be found in the joint senior leadership of Chemical Banking Corp. and Manufacturers Hanover Trust, who very decidedly chose to build a new culture encompassing the best of both rather than struggle for which might prevail, and took action to make that happen. In a joint venture, Texas Instruments and Hitachi consciously agreed to work on their cultural differences during the first year, particularly around their differences in decision-making processes.[5] Given that there was a lot to be gained by two

Exhibit 4-3. Requirements for approaching a culture change toward teams.

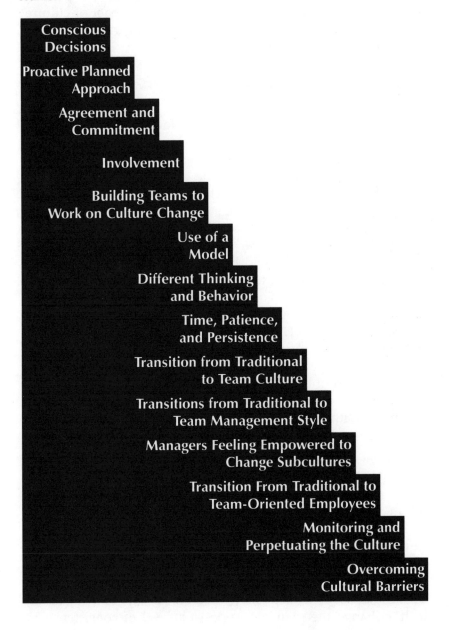

Conscious
Decisions

Proactive Planned
Approach

Agreement and
Commitment

Involvement

Building Teams to
Work on Culture Change

Use of a
Model

Different Thinking
and Behavior

Time, Patience,
and Persistence

Transition from Traditional
to Team Culture

Transitions from Traditional to
Team Management Style

Managers Feeling Empowered to
Change Subcultures

Transition From Traditional to
Team-Oriented Employees

Monitoring and
Perpetuating the Culture

Overcoming
Cultural Barriers

semiconductor makers' successfully joining forces and being a team, they chose to start slow and then enlarge their efforts. In all of these cases we see an awareness of the impact of culture on teams and teamwork, and vice versa, driving a conscious decision to address the issues involved.

Proactive Planned Approach

Culture change should be a proactive effort, thought about and planned rather than done piecemeal or as a stopgap measure in response to the problems that arise. It requires what we call "systems think" when planning the change. A manager must anticipate and consider how each change within the system, even a tiny one, impacts the other parts of the organization, including reporting relationships, departmental functions, policies, work interfaces, and even informal social structures.

A plan of action should be developed based on data collected about the culture (more specifically described in Chapter 6 on needs assessment). The plan must be tailored to the organization's tolerance to change and to constraints such as resources, flexibility, and time. The intent is to capitalize on and preserve the positive, supportive team aspects of the culture and address the inhibiting aspects. A series of steps and sequence of events need to be part of the plan of action, which serves as the guide for change as well as a road map publicized to organization members. Within each of the events, decision points and outcomes are based on the data and the needs of the organization.

Agreement and Commitment

The plan requires agreement on and commitment to the desired future culture and expected outcomes, as well as with the current culture and why it should change. This takes place at the senior level first and then throughout the organization. (The challenge of how to obtain agreement among key players is dealt with in subsequent chapters.) Needless to say, to embark on such a change the plan presupposes a level of consistency in thought, behavior, commitment, and energy.

Involvement

The culture change requires involvement of as many organization members as possible. Although this makes perfect sense, culture change has traditionally been assigned to the human resources department or to a special department given the task of accomplishing the mission, such as customer service, the quality department, or a culture change division. Relegating such a critical process to one department is fraught with difficulties and doomed to failure. It will remain just a program or overlay onto the current culture. Human resources departments, in their attempt to "enlighten" and facilitate organization change, usually take on the challenge, hoping to help while knowing their efforts will be futile.

Building Teams to Work on the Culture Change

What better opportunity is there to utilize teams than to revamp the company's culture so that it supports them? Creating the teams is the easy step. Actively building high performance to meet the challenge is a little more involved. The teams need to work not only on the various aspects of the culture to be adjusted but also on the way the teams function to achieve the goal. These teams must serve as positive role models for teamwork. In turn, proactively building the teams is important preparation for their journey. We have found that the key ingredients for success are clarifying expectations for high performance, giving feedback about the teams' strengths and weaknesses in meeting those expectations, and providing the needed skills while applying them to the culture change.

Use of a Model

Senior managers typically rely on their instincts, their personal styles, and what has worked in the past to effect culture change. We strongly recommend instead the use of a model, as described in the next chapters, which takes into account the senior managers' inclinations plus the requirements explored here. A structure is important and useful in ensuring that all of the cultural needs are attended to in a logical sequence.

Different Thinking and Behavior

Approaching a culture change to support teams requires different ways of thinking and different types of behaviors. These are far from profound and in fact are quite commonly described as effective management. Yet for many reasons, they are not practiced. In fact, some of the more basic truths or management tenets are outright ignored. We call them "lessons never learned," which any manager should reflect on if he or she is to be effective.

1. *Set goals.* How many times have you heard that if you don't have goals, you may not get there, or if you do arrive, you won't know it? Change requires direction. If your senior team, no less the organization, doesn't understand or agree upon the goals and direction, your chances of getting there are slim.

2. *Don't change just for change's sake.* Why are you changing? What do you hope to achieve? You must have a clear reason that is linked to your business strategy. If you can't define what you expect to occur as a result of teams, teamwork, and the new culture, you won't be able to see and realize the results.

3. *Tell people why the change is occurring.* People need to know the "why" in addition to the "what" of the change. Knowing that the organization has been restructured, merged, or had teams instituted for *general* reasons is not enough. And telling people it was done as a business necessity or in hopes of realizing increased productivity or market gains gives them only half the picture. They must be given the other half too, allowing them to understand more specifically why the change has occurred and how it creates new expectations of them regarding teamwork, results, etc. If your managers and staff are to be intelligent supporters and contributors to the change, they must be educated as to the expected returns.

4. *Realize that information is power.* How many times have you heard that? Data are critical in an effective change effort.

You need to know where the organization culture is today and what you want it to be in the future. Understanding the gaps helps to create a relevant plan. It enables you to preserve and capitalize on what is good and to address the negatives. Data can set you free from misconceptions and misdirected efforts.

5. *Walk the talk.* If teamwork is espoused and expected, senior managers clearly need to model that same behavior. "Do as I say, not as I do" won't work. Your actions will speak far louder than your words. Similarly, your management team needs to become an effective team and behave like one, in order to send the right messages about commitment to change.

6. *Recognize that you get what you measure and reward.* The most powerful statement an organization can make is what it measures, evaluates, and rewards. What people are held accountable for is what you will see achieved. This requires careful thought. Conversely, what is not measured and recognized will be considered unimportant. Teamwork, team results, and culture change progress are key components to be measured and rewarded.

7. *Select the right people.* Selection is the first step in an effective performance management system. Selecting the right people for the job can minimize the time and effort spent on performance problems. In a team culture, you need to hire and promote people who not only are competent but are compatible and reflect the new culture. Current selection criteria must change to ensure that.

8. *Tell people what is expected of them.* How can you hold people accountable for something when they don't know you expect them to do it? It's poor management to hope that they will somehow figure it out, or tell them what they didn't do but should have done. Culture change pushes everything back to ground zero. There is a greater need than ever before to provide clarity about what is expected.

9. *Appreciate people as your most valuable resources.* In practice, this requires organizations to foster mutual respect, teamwork among specialties and departments, and full appreciation of the internal-customer concept. It also requires that managers

truly value their people resources, empower them, and tap their expertise. Culture change toward teams requires these actions tenfold.

10. *Communicate, communicate, communicate.* This is the most overutilized word yet the most underutilized process. The importance of communication cannot be overstated. Major gaps typically exist, both vertically as well as laterally, in most companies. What is nice versus necessary to communicate gets confused or is evaluated by the individual having the information rather than the one needing the information. What is withheld unknowingly or out of protection varies with organizations' or managers' personalities. A culture change requires consistent and regular communication of what is nice *and* necessary about teamwork and the change.

11. *Cut your losses.* Organizations need to let go of people who are not performing or are not compatible with the company's culture. The amount of wasted time, energy, effort, and pain that goes into people who do not fit the job or the cultural requirements is far greater than the pain of letting them go. The message sent to others about what is expected is equally important. Yet organizations have continued to hold on, put nonperforming or incompatible employees "on a shelf," or shield them until recent pressures of downsizing gave them and the employees an out. A new team culture requires letting go of people who are not able to get on board after they've been given every opportunity.

These familiar "lessons never learned" are required for culture change. It means a different way of thinking and behaving. Perhaps the necessity to ensure success in such turbulent times will be the impetus to act on these long-standing management truths.

Time, Patience, and Persistence

A culture change takes time, patience, and persistence. It is not a quick fix or a "one minute manager" strategy. Most research states that it could take from five to ten years for an organization to actualize the new culture. We have found that with a planned, conscious effort, companies can achieve it in three to five years. Front-end planning expedites the change and short-circuits problems.

Realize that *achieving* the change means that you no longer talk about it, but rather it becomes the new way of doing business—the way of life in your company. Keep in mind that progress occurs and results are visible for each year of the culture change. But reaching the "natural way of life" phase takes three to five years, depending on how aggressively the company approaches the change.

Interestingly, companies are sometimes unaware that they have reached that phase. Attorneys' Title Insurance Fund in Florida is one example. During the company's fifth year into the culture change, at one of our follow-up meetings with the senior team, the members expressed a concern that people were no longer talking about the culture change as they once had. Yet management agreed that things were going terrifically: People were living up to what was expected, they were operating as a high-performing organization team, customer feedback was consistently positive, and the hoped-for results were surpassing their expectations. So what was wrong? Nothing; they were living the new culture. New employees never knew things had been different in the past. Longer-term employees remembered and truly appreciated the change of life at the Fund. The senior team began to fully appreciate that the culture change was achieved.

Culture change requires time, patience, and persistence. This goes against the natural corporate instinct of short-term, immediate results and quarterly profits. Just a little more staying power can wield a culture change with tremendous results.

Transition From a Traditional to a Team Culture

Historically, organizations were structured and functioned in particular ways that served them well. There are still many strong remnants of that in today's corporate cultures. Given the dynamic environment and demands imposed, traditional hierarchical cultures must make the transition to a dramatically different team-oriented culture, whose new requirements are depicted in Exhibit 4-4. Let's look at each requirement shown in the exhibit and then examine a few companies undergoing the transition.

Hierarchical to Flat

Most companies have been hierarchical, with multiple layers of management. They had strong boundaries between management and staff as well as between layers of management. Status was equated to the number of resources and mastery of people within one's own expertise. Decisions were centralized and tightly controlled. In contrast, organizations with team cultures are flatter and/or matrixed. Managerial demarcations and hierarchical boundaries are reduced. Status comes from the mastery of problems, situations, and skills across boundaries. Decision making is decentralized and more widespread.

Fragmentation to Cohesion

Silos have been created and maintained within traditional organizations. They may be based on departments, specialties, divisions, or locations. People develop a stovepipe mentality where they often don't remember the overarching company goal and how each area's role contributes to accomplishing it. Production or delivery of services has often been fragmented where there are "handoffs" to other silos, with no feeling of connectedness or responsibility for the result. Team cultures require a breaking down of those silos, with greater collaboration, inclusiveness, and coordination of stakeholders in planning, implementing, and evaluating results. There needs to be a greater willingness to share and shift resources and enhance interdepartmental teamwork. A smoother transition of handoffs and a continuum of services and product delivery requires greater appreciation of the bigger goal and each others' roles and contributions.

Exhibit 4-4. Transition from traditional to team cultures.

Traditional		Team
Hierarchical	→	Flat
↑	Layers	↓
↑	Boundaries	↓
↑	Centralized	↓
Fragmentation	→	Cohesion
↑	Silos	↓
↑	Handoffs	↓
↓	Responsibility	↑
↓	Collaboration	↑
↓	Coordination	↑
↓	Shift Resources	↑
Independence	→	Interdependence
↑	Individualism	↓
↓	Reliance on Others	↑
↓	Team Rewards	↑
↓	How vs. What	↑
Competition	→	Cooperation
↑	Myopia	↓
↓	Internal Customer	↑
↓	Partnership	↑
↓	Shared Resources and Information	↑
↓	Sacrifice for Broader Goal	↑
Tried-and-True	→	Risk Taking
↑	Past Success	↓
↑	Track Record	↓
↓	Ambiguity	↑
↓	Risk Taking	↑
↓	Creativity	↑
↓	Insecurity	↑

Note: Arrows pointing down indicate a decreased tendency; arrows pointing up indicate an increased tendency.

Independence to Interdependence

In the past, companies have sought out the consummate individual and encouraged behavior fostering the independence and autonomy of the individual expert and department. On the other hand, teaming requires an appreciation of interdependence: what it is and how it affects how one works. It means understanding when, for what, and how one maintains independence and functions accordingly, as well as when, for what, and how one acts dependently or relies on others. That means perhaps looking sideways more frequently in order to integrate and coordinate efforts. Similarly, it means that the organization must adjust and balance its recognition and rewards for this new team behavior along with the individual's accomplishments. How things are achieved—not just what—must be a valued part of the results.

Competition to Cooperation

Hierarchies, silos, and individualism have perpetuated competition among individuals, other departments, or other divisions. These have often been to the detriment of the customer. If the different parts of an organization are all striving to "win" or compete for resources, based on their myopic view of the world, customers do not get the best results from the overall organization's efforts. Team cultures require greater internal cooperation and sharing of information, resources, and power. The internal-customer concept should be fully understood as a critical strategy for improved overall organizational results and customer satisfaction. Team cultures embrace internal and external partnerships. Comfort in relying on others is a must. Cooperation, and perhaps sacrifice, in achieving the bigger goal needs to be rewarded.

Tried-and-True to Risk Taking

Organizations have often relied on tried-and-true successes: "If it worked in the past, it should work here!" "If it's not broken, why fix it?" There was a track record of experience and results that was heavily relied on to chart the future course or respond to roadblocks. Team cultures require greater comfort with ambiguity and exploring uncharted waters. What has worked in the past will not apply to the future. It is necessary to be able to take risks and be creative in solutions, to be confident enough to feel insecure while creating a new future.

Some Organizations in Transition

Bell Labs is one example of an organization in transition. The company needed to change its culture from one that reinforced the tradition of specialization, focusing on individual projects and technological achievement within a particular department, to one that had more of an outward focus toward the customer. It adjusted by giving broader assignments rather than those based on the employee's narrow technological specialization. Researchers were assigned to business units and had greater access to customers. They were all required to spend more time interacting sideways, internally, and with their customers.[6]

A customer mandate forced Mobil Oil's research and engineering departments to improve their coordination in providing services and technology. At one point the organization created an informal organization of what were called focus teams to accomplish this. These were middle management teams with both the research and engineering sides represented. Their mission was to jointly manage technology areas internally and externally to ensure improved partnership and results. The focus teams were overseen by a senior management team called the Manufacturing Team. The concept worked extremely well. It broke down traditional research and engineering boundaries and created tremendous synergies.

A merger between two pharmaceutical companies, Bristol Myers and Squibb, and the resulting clash between their original cultures, was another impetus for change. One company had an open, participative culture that encouraged employee input and decision making. The other company's culture had a bottom line emphasis, a strict chain-of-command hierarchy, and a top-down, disciplined approach to problem solving. It was inevitable that these two cultures would clash, as they did in one division that was in the critical path for new-drug development. Rather than attempt to continuously resolve conflicts, the leader of the division decided to blend the best of the two cultures into a new culture that used teams. The division was the first in Bristol-Myers Squibb to overcome the culture clash, and it became a model for other divisions in the new company.

When Coca-Cola's CEO Roberto Goizueta took over in 1981, his challenge was to create change in the comfortable and bureaucratic culture. He took numerous steps to stimulate movement within the company. He asked questions and changed protocol at meetings. He described what jobs could be decentralized. However, as he pushed the culture for greater acceptance of change, he was careful not to denigrate the past. He proselytized about the importance and need to change. *Fortune* quoted him as saying, "Don't wrap the flag of Coca-Cola around you to prevent change from taking place." He followed through by continuing to urge change as he continued to make dramatic changes.[7]

Transition From a Traditional to a Team Management Style

The management style for a team culture needs to be different from the styles ingrained in classic hierarchical organizations. This includes the styles of managers, whether they be in charge of a department, division, project or ad hoc team, or matrix. Although teams and structural changes have been installed in many organizations, the command-and-control management style has carried over from previous days. Although that style may have been successful in the past, it will not work well in nor promote the necessary team environment. Exhibit 4-5 depicts some of the requirements for making the transition from a traditional to a team management style. (Note that arrows in the figure point up or down to indicate increased or decreased tendencies.)

Command-and-control is a comfortable style. Decisions and information are tightly controlled, and delegation, if done at all, is done judiciously with tight controls to ensure success. The manager or leader tends to be the hub of all activity, demonstr-

Exhibit 4-5. Transition from traditional to team style.

Command-and-Control Style		Team Style
↑	Tight Control	↓
↓	Shared Responsibility	↑
↓	Delegation	↑
↓	Empowerment	↑
↑	Manager as the Hub	↓
↓	Information Sharing	↑
↑	Autocratic	↓
↑	Distance	↓
↓	Evaluate Process and Results	↑

Note: Arrows pointing down indicate a decreased tendency; arrows pointing up indicate an increased tendency.

ating autocratic behavior by what and how directions are given and communication shared. There is a conscious distance created in the relationship between the leader and staff. Trust issues are often an obstacle to empowering team members and staff. The leader usually feels solely responsible for the success of the team or department. Typically, the command-and-control leader focuses on results without consideration of the process that the team or department has used to achieve the results.

The new team culture requires a major shift toward sharing responsibility, decision making, and information. This means that leaders need to let go of control, empower employees, and delegate previously tightly controlled responsibility and authority. They must become integrators and coordinators of activity who think about and consistently remind others about their interdependencies.

Team styles foster commitment and self-direction rather than reliance on the leader. Shared responsibility for the success of the team is promoted. The leader stays in the team loop but does not *become* the loop, and leaders must remain confident of the team or department's ability to succeed with or without them. The new orientation focuses on and evaluates the process of teamwork as well as results achieved.

As logical as they may sound, these characteristics are not easily actualized. To do so requires very different ways of thinking and behaving, as well as new leadership skills and techniques that training can provide. It also requires holding leaders accountable for changing to a new leadership style. In some instances, replacing those leaders who are unable to adjust and let go of what has worked for them in the past may be the only alternative.

Feeling Empowered to Change Subcultures

Managers often feel powerless to change their environment. They feel victim to a larger corporate culture and assign any hope of change to the CEO or the most senior manager of their organization. Similarly, managers are often unaware of their own power to create or change their current subculture. They do not realize or take credit for the fact that they have created their own unique environment, which may or may not support teams and teamwork. If they underestimate the power they had to create their own subculture, they clearly underestimate their power to change it.

Another issue that influences managers' feelings of empowerment is that culture is perceived as difficult to change (as discussed in Chapter 3). In addition, managers have never been given skills or a process for going about creating culture or subculture change. The lack of understanding about how to revamp their culture to support teams compounds their feelings of powerlessness and inhibits their confidence to act.

Transition From Traditional to Team-Oriented Employees

The employee style for a team culture needs to be different from the deeply ingrained attitudes and behaviors perpetuated by the traditional hierarchical organization. This includes employees in general as well as team members. Just as the managerial styles of the past have carried over, so too has employee conditioning.

Many employees and team members resent the command-and-control style still being practiced. Yet they too have fallen into a comfortable and safe pattern of behavior we call the traditional employee syndrome. They wait for direction and don't initiate unless their leader pushes them. They are quick to relinquish responsibility for work and results to the leader, rather than share responsibility. They are not forthcoming with concerns or questions, but they complain that the leader hasn't told them or given them something they needed. Some point fingers and complain about management and "what a joke this teamwork or empowerment thing is." Others carry around tremendous anger about it. Many have become noncontributors, keeping a low profile and hoping they will be left alone.

Keep in mind that many of these employee behaviors are occurring not only in environments where traditional styles prevail but also in ones where things have changed. There are countless examples of employees overtly and subtly fighting the change and the new expectations being imposed on them in a team culture.

The new team culture requires that they contribute, initiate action, ask questions, solve problems, and share responsibility for the success of the team, department, and organization. It requires that they own their behavior and become team players rather than individual experts operating in a vacuum. It means improving their coordination, communication, and decision making within the context of a department, team, or multiple teams. The bottom line is that they must become more accountable for what and how they do things and for sharing responsibility for the culture change. They must overcome the fear and insecurity that is stimulated by being held accountable. They also need to overcome their feelings of powerlessness in order to create change. Given the historical patterns of behavior and relationships between the manager and employee, it is important that they give each other support during the transition. The change in culture requires a journey for all organization members.

Monitoring and Perpetuating the Culture

As difficult as it is to change a culture, it must also be maintained and perpetuated. Once strategies are in place and it becomes the way of life in the organization, the new culture takes on a force of its own. Monitoring and following up to ensure that it continues to work and achieve the expected results is critical.

Intermittent checks are important, done by senior management or an ad hoc or permanent transition team whose primary role is to take the pulse of the culture. This involves monitoring how the established systems are working to support teams, managerial and staff attitudes and behaviors, and the results being achieved. A conscious effort is important to ensure a new culture's longevity and continued success.

When the auto manufacturer Saturn built its culture from scratch, the first ninety-nine employees helped create it. They were risk takers who came together to create a new company. They built their own procedures, identified suppliers, and planned the future. Their energy and enthusiasm for the vision were powerful forces in creating and perpetuating the culture at first. However, when others joined the company, there was no time to integrate them into the culture; they had to get to work. There was no time or effort put forth to educate them about the history or what the culture was, nor to sweep them into the energy force initiated by the creators of the culture. One year later, though, Saturn realized it needed to step back and make up for that oversight.

The coffee company Starbucks is an example of a very powerful culture with deep-rooted values and commensurate behaviors. The employees' spirit of teamwork manifests itself in a philosophy of treating each other and customers with respect and dignity. A "Howardism," as employees call it—taken from CEO Howard Schultz—is that if we serve the best coffee in the world, how we treat people should be the same. There is a corporate conscience of doing for the greater good, as demonstrated by Starbucks donating to CARE and funding projects to help coffee-producing countries. The company takes great pride in its culture. However, because it has grown from 11 stores in 1987 to 700 stores today and anticipates 2,000 stores in the year 2000, the greatest concern is how to replicate and perpetuate the culture. The company is consciously planning how to do so, given the powerful force of Howard Schultz and the limited exposure to him that future employees would have. Something that has helped Starbucks monitor and perpetuate the culture is a daily cultural audit, called a Mission Review Audit. This is a system that allows anyone to write up a concern about any policy, manager, or employee behavior that does not support the mission and values, and send it to the appropriate corporate office. Action is always taken on the audits.

All cultures need nurturing, whether created by a new company, one that has been around awhile, or one that has recently changed its culture. It is important to be aware of this and take conscious steps to do it.

Overcoming Deep-Rooted Cultural Barriers

Creating a culture that supports teams requires overcoming deep-rooted cultural barriers within yourself and others. Let's examine some of them.

Teams vs. the Individual

Teamwork is defined as "work done by a number of associates all subordinating personal prominence for the good of the whole." The words that jump out and grab you in the gut are probably "subordinating personal prominence." This is antithetical to everything we have been taught to believe in our lives. Inherent in American culture are values such as individuality, independence, competition, and winning—a far cry from "subordinating." Education further reinforces these values by training people in individual specialties and professions to operate independently and often with a myopic perspective of their work. There is little attempt to educate us about the interdependence of other specialties or how to work together to accomplish an overall goal. In our work lives, organizations then perpetuate the silos and individuality orientation by placing people in distinct and often isolated departments that tend to compete with each other for resources and for glory. And finally, managers and employees have been historically rewarded for their individual accomplishment, not that of "the team," whether it be a project, departmental, or organizational team. In fact, many organizations call employees "individual contributors."

This helps us understand why we struggle with the concept of teamwork, which should be like motherhood and apple pie. Instead, it is in strong contrast to deep-seated American beliefs and values. However, the transition can be eased somewhat if we think about "subordinating" within a team context in tangible behavioral ways. Subordinating in a team means things like sometimes listening rather than speaking, being open to others' ideas, compromising, sharing or giving others credit, and sharing blame. These are important behaviors for any type of team, but they require a lot of effort, given our habits thus far. If reward systems support these behaviors, there is a greater impetus for change.

A 1995 study sponsored by the American Society for Quality Control, Disney, General Motors, Kellogg's, and Kodak supports this observation about the cultural clash. It found that the need for individual recognition and growth clashed with team requirements; the study suggested that both the group and individual needs should be dealt with in order for teams to be successful.

Interdependence

The need to understand and operate interdependently, as described earlier, is another contradiction to our values of independence. The term implies knowing when to function independently and when to be dependent on others, appreciating the interrelationship in producing an overall product or service. People can overreact to this concept by becoming totally reliant, relinquishing all independence, or going to the other extreme of being totally autonomous and refusing to actively participate. "OK, just tell me what to do" versus "I'll do my own thing until someone notices" are reflective of the potential backlash to teaming, with other reactions being somewhere on the continuum between independence and interdependence.

Overcoming Lessons Never Learned

The "lessons never learned" that we reviewed earlier in this chapter apply to managers holding on for dear life to their habitual ways of thinking and behaving. Even though we cling to those habits, we continue to search for solutions, fads, reinventions, and repackaged concepts in hopes of finding the key. We look for quick fixes, charismatic leaders, or cheerleading themes, with the fantasy that teams and culture change can perhaps be as simple as the one-minute-manager remedy. We *try* to change, but somehow our energy gets diverted to the most pressing issue of the day. Then of course there is the energy, time, and pain of having to discard what we know and do in order to become different.

Reactive vs. Proactive

Another deep-seated American societal and corporate cultural value is that we are reactive. We respond quickly to pain. Organizations are forced to react to competition, losing market share, out-of-whack budgets, or survival issues. Dramatic change in today's organizations is often only a result of a problem.

As an example, health care in the United States has always been curative rather than preventive, in both treatment of patients as well as management perspective. Today, because of the economic and business environment's demands, skyrocketing costs, and tremendous competition, health care has responded by focusing on prevention, managed care, and alliances.

The "don't fix it unless it's broken" mentality has pervaded most organizations, where anticipating and preventing problems or proactively addressing challenges has not been a norm. This reactive mode is closely aligned with the short-term focus of organizations. Quarterly profits, quick fixes, the big hits, and immediate results are all part of the mind-set. Sacrificing the short term for the long term and waiting for returns on investments are hard pills to swallow.

Preconceptions That Sabotage Action

Many of the preconceptions and myths about culture, teamwork, and change, previously described in Chapter 2, end up creating false hopes and reinforcing inaction. For example, if managers believe that teamwork will occur naturally or just through training, in spite of the environment, they will not own responsibility for the change. They will sabotage their own and their department's or team's success. Dispelling those myths may not be comfortable, but it is imperative.

The different thinking and behavior required for a team culture will not occur overnight for managers and employees. It takes time and nurturing. There will be some who can't adapt, no matter how hard they try. There will be others who will not change, no matter how hard *you* try. It's important that both managers and employees be aware of this when judging whether the organization and person are no longer compatible.

Say vs. Do

There is often a major gap between what managers say and what they do. Sometimes there truly is a blind spot about the void. Other times, perhaps we hope no one will notice. But of course, everyone does. We can't espouse teamwork and not model team behavior yet expect it of others. A recent Towers Perrin study found that the majority of executives cited people as their most valuable asset and stated that their enhanced performance would affect the company's bottom line. However, the executives then ranked people-oriented strategies lower than result-oriented strategies as a way to ensure company success.[8] This illustrates a disconnection between what is said and done. There tends to be a recurring neglect of *how* organizations go about achieving the *what*. Teams and culture fall into that same pattern. They are critical for improved results yet are often not linked as critical strategies to attend to.

Resistance to Change

The natural human resistance to change only compounds how deep-seated many of these societal or organizational cultural barriers are. The definition of change in and of itself is enough to scare anyone, since change "implies an essential difference, sometimes amounting to a loss of original identity or a substitution of one thing for another" (Webster's New Collegiate Dictionary). There are many emotions triggered when changing from a traditional to a team-oriented style and culture. Reactions include feeling powerless due to loss of control, insecurity about future competence and ability to function in the new culture, uncertainty about job security, and anger about the change and having to face the fact that the old ways won't work today. Change also creates anxiety about the time, effort, and personal adjustments to be made. Resistance and reactions to change must be expected and managed. Managers and employees must be empathetic to their mutual fears associated with the change. They must help each other in the transition.

Notes

1. Gene G. Marcial, "The Wachovia and Suntrust Tango," *Business Week,* October 9, 1995.

2. "The Case Against Mergers," Special Report, *Business Week,* October 30, 1995.

3. Karen Lowry Miller et al.,"The Toughest Job in Europe," *Business Week,* October 9, 1995.

4. Mark Maremont, "Kodak's New Focus," *Business Week,* January 30, 1995.

5. Neal Templin, "Strange Bedfellows," *The Wall Street Journal,* November 1, 1995.

6. "New Paths to Success," *Fortune,* June 12, 1995.

7. Betsy Morris, "Roberto Goizueta and Jack Welch: The Wealth Builders," *Fortune,* December 11, 1995.

8. Barbara Presley Noble, "The Bottom Line on 'People' Issues," *The New York Times,* February 19, 1995.

5

A Culture Change Model for Success

The future does not get better by hope, it gets better by plan.

—Jim Rohn

Companies responding to their challenges by implementing teams have often been unsuccessful. They have been faced with project teams that are not producing the expected results, divisions in the same company duplicating efforts when serving clients, newly created team matrix structures that are not working, and severe conflict and a lack of teamwork within a department in a newly merged company.

As consultants called upon to deal with these problems, we devised what we call the Organization Culture Change Model. Models are instrumental in the art and practice of leadership and management. They provide consistency and structure in addressing organizational issues, are the context for logical action, and help to ensure success.

This chapter introduces the Change Model and describes its six essential parts (shown in Exhibit 5-1), which any organization has to address if its culture is to be successfully changed. The six components, the topics of extended discussion in the next six chapters, are treated briefly here to provide an overview.

Exhibit 5-1. The six essential parts of creating culture change.

1. Needs Assessment

2. Executive Direction

3. Infrastructure

4. Collateral Organizations

5. Training

6. Evaluation

© 1988 Corporate Management Developers, Inc.

An Overview of the Model

We'll start with a quick look at each of the six components of the Culture Change Model.

Needs Assessment

The first component is called Needs Assessment. Most organizations are unable to describe their existing culture or the one to which they aspire. Sometimes senior management assumes that the existing culture is supportive of teams, while employees feel the opposite. But neither can articulate specifically what the current culture is or how it should change.

So an essential first step is a process of data gathering and analysis to determine the gaps in culture between the current and the desired. The Needs Assessment serves to identify:

1. How employees feel about the change to formalized teams
2. What current organization processes and systems are in place
3. How those systems may either support or hinder the new culture
4. What processes or systems are missing but required to support the change
5. What obstacles exist to implementing the new culture
6. Positive aspects of the current culture to preserve

In determining how employees feel about the change to formalize teams, it's important to know that they often view it as the "program of the month" and don't take it seriously. It's important to identify current processes and systems because, for example, in numerous cases the performance appraisal system focuses on individual contributions rather than teamwork, and such a system obviously needs to be changed. Existing communications systems, such as incompatible e-mail or management directives prohibiting communication across organizational boundaries, often hinder how teams operate.

The data gathered during the Needs Assessment phase are analyzed and used when working with the senior management team during the Executive Direction Retreat.

Executive Direction

The second component of the model is Executive Direction. Most organizations need to be much more focused and directive regarding *where* they are going with their new culture about teams and *why* it is important to get there. The lack of clear focus is often interpreted by organization members to mean ambivalence or worse: "They don't know where they're going or what they're doing." Recent examples are organizations that have embarked on quality or customer service initiatives because "it's the right thing to do" rather than specifying the real reasons, such as increasing market share or ensuring survival in a more competitive environment.

Definitive steps must be taken by management to articulate

to the organization a clear, unified, unambiguous direction. When management is in agreement about this new direction, it becomes the driving force for changing the organization's culture toward teamwork.

The Executive Direction product is typically the result of a two- or three-day retreat for the executive-level managers. The retreat is designed to obtain their agreement about the direction of the organization and to provide focus for the culture change toward teams. It also serves to build the executive team so that its members serve as role models for change. During the retreat, a number of products are generated, including a statement of philosophy about teams and teamwork, which becomes the foundation for defining new expectations of the organization. The executive team members also develop Standards for Success, which reflect what they expect to achieve by the culture change. These are measurable outcomes that the team will monitor and evaluate as a barometer of success. The Standards for Success become the impetus for action-planning changes in behavior and processes that will lead to implementing the culture change toward teams. Other products are developed as needed to meet the circumstances in each organization. These products are used later in the process to align the infrastructures and provide input for the training and evaluation phases of the model.

Infrastructure

The third component of the model treats the infrastructure of the organization. The Infrastructure is composed of processes and systems that make any organization function smoothly (or not), such as the selection system, performance management system, and recognition system. All have to be changed and aligned to support the new team culture. For instance, organizations that hire or promote the consummate individual while espousing teamwork are sending the wrong message. So is rewarding and celebrating individuals and not teams, which creates confusion for employees who are operating in a formal teaming structure.

There are hundreds of examples of how the infrastructure in organizations works against formalizing teams. Think of a

time when you attended company training and learned an exciting, breakthrough concept, only to return to your old environment that didn't support the new concept. How can there be
positive change under such circumstances? A supportive infrastructure is a key to the success of change, yet it is paid the least
attention in most organizations.

Infrastructure and its component parts are shown in Exhibit
5-2; they are discussed in more detail in Chapter 8. Suffice it to
say here that "tweaking" (that is, the making of changes in) the
infrastructure processes and systems is a crucial step in ensuring
success in the culture change toward teamwork.

Collateral Organizations

The fourth part of the model refers to collateral organizations:
temporary organizational structures that are sometimes used in
the change process. These temporary groups have the specific
task of helping to implement the culture change by working on
the parts of the infrastructure that require attention. The members of the collateral organization also play the important role of
ambassadors of the culture change within the corporation.

Training

The fifth part of the model deals with training. Change of any
magnitude usually entails training—and certainly the change to
formalized teams is no exception. If companies pay the least attention to the infrastructure, then they tend to pay the most attention to training. Many organizations *do* invest in training for
teams, but we also find that often training is *all* they invest in,
usually ignoring the other components of the model. Hours of
team training are expended, and often wasted, because the Executive Direction is unclear or the systems haven't been tweaked
to support the training that participants receive.

Training can take a number of avenues, but the most successful makes the training a limited intervention for each group
of participants. We have found that rather than give general
training on working in teams to everyone, it's better to have actual team building of intact teams. This gives the intact, formal-

Exhibit 5-2. The Organization Culture Change Model.

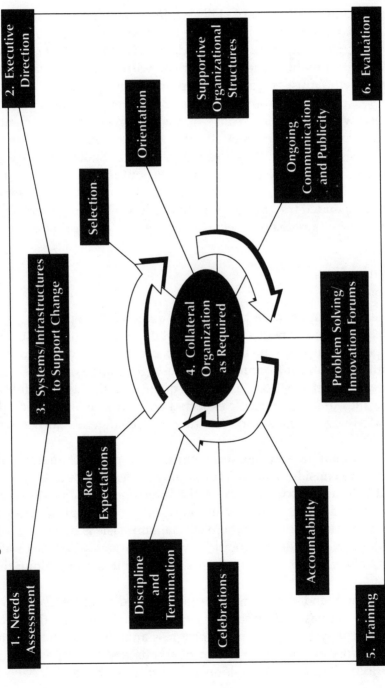

1. Needs Assessment
2. Executive Direction
3. Systems/Infrastructures to Support Change
4. Collateral Organization as Required
5. Training
6. Evaluation

Selection
Orientation
Role Expectations
Supportive Organizational Structures
Discipline and Termination
Celebrations
Accountability
Problem Solving/Innovation Forums
Ongoing Communication and Publicity

ized teams the necessary skills while also giving them a jump-start to success. It deals with the real team issues rather than a generic formula. Team building deals with the entire team and all of its unique issues rather than with an individual team leader who must go back and apply the concepts alone.

Usually, data from the Needs Assessment and the results of work with the senior team—decisions, products, agreements, and plans—are fed back to the trainees. This information becomes the impetus for their own change. Skills necessary to succeed in a team environment round out the training for employees. In general, managers and team leaders attend a separate, expanded training session that includes building their skills to manage their teams effectively in the new environment.

Evaluation

The last component of the model is Evaluation. Typically, organizations tend to neglect this concept of defining and measuring expected outcomes in the change process. They often wait for some outcomes to occur, or they use generalities such as "increased efficiency" or "improved quality" rather than defining specific outcomes. Specific expected outcomes should reflect the underlying reasons for initiating the change to formalized teams.

Evaluation and measurement are critical to changing culture. We consider evaluation not only a means to assess results but also a component part of the intervention itself. Measurement and continued communication of in-progress results serve to pinpoint areas where special emphasis is needed. They also provide feedback about how far an organization has traveled along the journey to success and how it is doing along the way.

The Standards for Success generated during the Executive Direction phase define specific expected outcomes and the measurement systems to monitor progress and success. These measurements are put in the form of trends and are reported out periodically to all stakeholders in the culture change.

Success in Using the Model

The Organization Culture Change Model has been used success-fully by a large number of organizations in their efforts to change their cultures to support teams. It has proven to have the flexibility required to be effective across industries and in a variety of situations. This flexibility extends to using the model when working with subcultures within a larger company's corporate culture.

For example, the model was used when working with two different groups in Bristol-Myers Squibb's Chemical Process Development Division, which had just undergone a merger. The two groups were experiencing many issues related to employees' not working well together. Management expressed the desire to institutionalize teams as the method to get work accomplished effectively. However, management's direction and expectations were not clearly and forcefully communicated. Although teams were formed, they were not functioning well. When the Change Model was applied, the Needs Assessment revealed that infrastructure issues had not been addressed and that employees did not possess the skills necessary to ensure successful teamwork. Management was educated about the need to administer to the corporate culture (or subculture in this case), and they applied the model to do so. Results included implementation of successful cross-divisional teams, reduced conflict, and increased efficiency. The process has become an example of how to implement teams throughout the company.

Another example of employing the model in a subculture was its use in the research and engineering departments of Mobil Oil. A subculture was created that supported formalized interdepartmental teams, which was distinctly different from how the departments had operated historically. The turf wars, conflict issues, and infrastructure problems that had developed were addressed by applying the model. The process resulted in cost savings and increased customer satisfaction, and it is currently being emulated in other parts of the company.

An example of applying the model successfully to an overall corporate culture is an effort recently completed with Attorneys' Title Insurance Fund, Florida's largest title insurance company. In this case, the company president wanted to create a companywide culture change to build the organization into a team that had better customer service as its goal. Results have been dramatic, including increased market share, reduced employee turnover, and increased customer satisfaction.

These examples indicate the overall model's utility and flexibility in changing corporate culture or subcultures to support teams. Now let's take a look at the specifics of the model.

The Detailed Model and Its Application

Exhibit 5-2 introduces the detailed Organization Culture Change Model. It depicts the specific systems within an organization's infrastructure that need to be in place and supportive of a culture change to a more formal use of teams. Chapters 6 through 11 describe each component of the model in detail, giving examples of a variety of companies in different industries and how they employed the model to implement culture change.

Many companies have used the model, but three in particular are followed throughout the book and introduced here. IBM's Q&IT (Quality and Information Technology division) and Mobil Oil's REEA (Research, Engineering, and Environmental Affairs departments) are examples of changing subcultures within the larger context of a major company. Attorneys' Title Insurance Fund is an example of changing the culture of an entire company.

IBM's Q&IT

IBM's Quality and Information Technology (Q&IT) organization provides services to internal customers within the North America Sales Organization. Q&IT was reorganized into a modified matrix organization. Essentially, all workers report to Competency Center Managers (CCMs), who have responsibility for the "care and feeding" of the Q&IT workforce. The CCMs provide training, career management, salary administration, discipline, counseling, performance review, and all other administrative and human resources support to the workforce. All employees (except at the executive level) report to a CCM.

Work in Q&IT is managed by Business Area Leaders (BALs). These BALs are designated as leaders for projects or a set of work-related duties. BALs are absolved of any personnel-related duties (the CCMs take care of that) and are able and expected to concentrate fully on getting the job done, although they are active participants in the process.

The competency centers consist of employees who are categorized, usually by skill or specialty, but sometimes by geographic location. Employees are assigned from the competency center to work on a project or projects as their skills are needed. Once their skills are no longer needed, they return to the competency center for reassignment.

This matrix is overseen by an executive group, each member of whom has responsibility for a specific function of the business. The executive group reports to a vice-president for Q&IT.

After a pilot was run in part of the organization, the matrix was implemented throughout Q&IT. The Organization Culture Change Model was used to change the Q&IT culture to accept and support the new teaming structure (the matrix). Subsequent chapters follow the Q&IT journey.

Mobil Oil's REEA

Mobil Oil's Research, Engineering, and Environmental Affairs (REEA) provided research and engineering services to other major divisions within the company such as Marketing and Refining (M&R), Exploration and Producing (E&P), and Mobil Chemical. Initially, REEA comprised separate functions in long-term research, near-term research and development, and engineering. Over the past few years, REEA's functions have been brought more and more into the same fold, until today REEA has been dramatically changed into the Mobil Technology Company (MTC). MTC provides similar services but with much more synergy than the old REEA.

The following chapters detail the evolution of REEA into MTC, a journey that took several phases. It began with the computer applications groups on both the research side and the engineering side. In an attempt to move in a new direction of more collaboration between research and engineering, which had been in conflict, CADET teams (for Computer Application Development Teams) were set up as the first interdivisional effort crossing boundaries between research and engineering. The CADET teams proved so successful that the effort was broadened, leading to the development of focus teams, which managed technology areas across research and engineering. These focus teams were led by a Manufacturing Team and an Executive Leadership Team (ELT), which brought the customer as a partner into the research and engineering arena. The evolution has continued such that today MTC is now one entity with research and engineering combined as one function that works in a matrixed structure to bring services to the M&R, E&P, and Mobil Chemical partners.

Attorneys' Title Insurance Fund

The Fund is headquartered in Orlando and has numerous branches around the state of Florida. A few years ago, its market share began to dwindle, going from about 22 percent down to 17 percent. This was caused by new competition from out-of-state companies trying to establish themselves in Florida. In a regulated industry, the Fund couldn't differentiate its service through pricing, so it decided to differentiate through better customer service.

The Customer Service Excellence (CSE) program was begun. The Fund began to view the company as a team that must provide excellent service to its constituency, and the Fund used a teaming concept in changing its culture. It formed a series of action teams that were managed by a Steering Committee, which reported to a Customer Service Executive Group (CSEG). The following chapters describe the culture change efforts of the Fund through the use of this team structure.

6

Using the Model: Needs Assessment

To be conscious that you are ignorant of the facts is a great step to knowledge.

—Benjamin Disraeli

The first step in the culture change process is conducting a Needs Assessment, which is highlighted in the overall Change Model shown in Exhibit 6-1. This step basically assesses the current corporate culture or subculture against the desired future team-oriented culture. It takes a snapshot of what currently exists in the environment, providing a baseline on what helps or hinders the organization in achieving its desired goals for teams. As such, it educates the organization about the scope of change needed and the commitment required to get where it wants to go. It also focuses management's thinking and helps management decide on the best strategies to adopt, stimulating their action planning and even serving as a motivator and impetus for change.

The Needs Assessment has two core elements, illustrated in Exhibit 6-2. The first is a cultural assessment of the culture or the subculture that is adopting teams. The second is a team effectiveness assessment. Each element has various dimensions, which are examined and discussed in detail in this chapter.

The primary aim of the Needs Assessment phase is to estab-

Exhibit 6-1. The Needs Assessment phase of the Organization Culture Change Model.

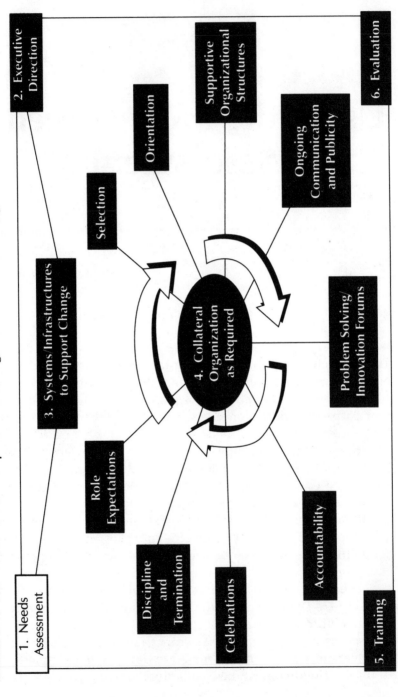

Exhibit 6-2. The two core elements of the Needs Assessment phase.

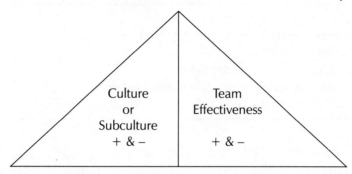

lish a baseline of what is positive and supportive as well as what is negative and inhibiting regarding teams in the culture. Identifying and publicizing what is positive in the environment and needs to be preserved is crucial in facilitating culture change. You have probably been in situations where "the new" supersedes and clouds the good aspects of "the old." Instead of discarding the old outright, organizations must promote and build upon the good from the past, identifying and nurturing those core values, principles, and practices within the culture that facilitate teams.

On the other hand, obstacles within the current culture need to be identified as well. Many organizations do not deal with problems proactively, instead ignoring impediments until they jump out and become major problems. This is certainly true when companies are instituting teams or undergoing the culture change process. It is imperative in the early stages to acknowledge and address any obstacles within the culture, such as core values, practices, and issues that hinder teams in order to devise targeted strategies to overcome them.

This chapter shows you how to conduct a Needs Assessment, beginning with descriptions of the cultural and team effectiveness assessments and going on to a discussion of step-by-step procedures to follow in your own organization.

Cultural Assessment

The cultural element of the assessment examines six dimensions of the environment, as shown in Exhibit 6-3.

Exhibit 6-3. The six dimensions of the cultural assessment.

1. Values/Beliefs/Behavioral Norms
2. Measurements Currently Being Used
3. Management Styles and Practices
4. Employee Styles and Behaviors
5. Infrastructures (Systems/Policies/Procedures)
6. Level of Understanding and Agreement About the Team Concept

These probably look familiar since they reflect many of the elements of a culture and of the Change Model.

Values, Beliefs, and Behavioral Norms

The first dimension of the cultural assessment is examining the values, beliefs, and behavioral norms that exist, against what might be needed in a team-oriented culture. For example, team cultures require values and behaviors that reflect:

- Positive internal relationships (internal customers) as well as positive external relationships (external customers)
- An emphasis on *how* something is accomplished as well as what is accomplished
- "Out of the box" thinking and, in turn, risk taking
- Confrontation of issues
- An appreciation of differences
- Proactive and long-term thinking
- Balanced respect for the individual and the team

Questions need to be posed that evaluate these values and practices:

- Are company values and practices linked to the individual, to the team, or to results?
- Is it how you achieve the goals that counts, or just the fact that you achieve them, regardless of how?
- Is the internal customer understood and valued as much as the external customer?

▸ Are risk taking and innovation encouraged, and are mistakes tolerated?
▸ What messages are reinforced verbally and behaviorally about quality, efficiency, empowerment, and teamwork?

The answers to these questions have cultural implications since they support or thwart high-performance teams and thus need to be addressed.

The following real-life examples illustrate various cultural values, beliefs, and behavioral norms and their impact on teaming.

The Internal Customer

The belief and related behaviors that the internal customer was unimportant interfered in Attorneys' Title Insurance Fund's attempt to get employees to see themselves as an organizational team to improve customer service. The members of each branch and department viewed themselves as distinct entities serving their own customer. They rarely viewed members of other departments as being on their team or helping them achieve their goals. As a matter of fact, some saw other departments as getting in their way. The norm was to blame others for not achieving good customer service, and managers reinforced this belief. The internal-customer concept was going to be a major cultural obstacle to teamwork for the Fund if it was not addressed by the senior management team.

Short-Term vs. Long-Term

Valuing short-term management responsiveness and crisis-oriented behavior took precedence over achieving longer-term improvement at Rohm & Haas, a major international chemical company that was embarking on a Total Quality Leadership Program utilizing teams as the primary vehicle for change and addressing key customer issues. In one particular division, everyone traveled extensively to solve customer problems. The division members never met as a team, rationalizing that they had to travel because their customers came first. This short-term focus obviously inhibited their ability to have ongoing teams to deal with the larger, high-impact customer-quality issues. Some trade-off had to be made if the company was to achieve its longer-term team goals.

Contrast this company culture with that of another organization that chose to value and foster the longer-term view for teams. Knowing that responsiveness to the customer was important, the company organized what it called "tiger teams" to deal with the immediate crises, while the other teams dealt with the long-term, high-impact customer issues.

Risk Taking

How two organizations' cultures encourage team creativity and react to mistakes determines their future regarding risk taking. At the *Fort Lauderdale Sun-Sentinel,* management expected out-of-the-box thinking from teams and risk taking, but such behavior was not the norm. In fact, employees were fearful of taking risks (in large part because of the editor's strong, forceful personality), and people continued to do things the same way. Contrast this culture with that at Multigraphics, an Illinois reprographics company, where the executive demanded creativity and risk taking. He pushed employees for new ideas and consistently demonstrated his displeasure at their lack of creative thinking. His motto was, "If it's not broken, it must not be working hard enough." Employees understood that to mean "Don't wait for it to be broken!" The teams at Multigraphics proactively came up with a lot of new ideas.

Valuing Differences

In some team environments, valuing differences and behaving that way can be a major challenge. In highly technical industries, degrees and pedigrees are strongly valued, which has created a history of superiority, hierarchy, and conflict between various groups such as research versus engineering, Ph.D.'s versus technicians, or M.D.'s versus nurses. These values and behavioral norms make it harder to establish equal playing grounds for team members; such norms need to be addressed since they will not just disappear. Holy Cross Hospital in Fort Lauderdale instituted interdisciplinary team building to help all employees fully appreciate one another's contribution, regardless of such things as background or rank.

These examples illustrate how corporate values, beliefs, and behavioral norms can be powerful forces in organization culture. Assessing this dimension helps to distinguish what works for or against teams' success, and what needs to be proactively identified and addressed during the Executive Direction retreat and subsequent events (discussed in detail in Chapter 7).

Measurements Currently Being Used

The second dimension of the cultural assessment is finding out what measurements are currently being used and how they are being used—information that helps identify what is valued by the organization. In a team culture, it is important that measures be defined and that they reflect the organization's goals for the team concept. In other words, what is the organization hoping to achieve or expecting from its teams? Is it customer satisfaction, innovation, revenue, productivity? In a team culture, measurement should be used as a barometer of success and to educate team and organization members about their progress toward the company's team goals.

The following questions need to be asked about the measurement dimension:

- What are teams being evaluated on?
- What is expected of you, and what are you held accountable for?
- How does your organization measure team success? How does it use the data?

The answers have important implications for what the senior team may need to decide, since you often get what you measure. For example, one telecommunications organization was measuring the number of projects and teams people worked on when it was really interested in the quality of the product and the impact on the bottom line. In another case, an organization was measuring whether team projects were on schedule and within budget. Although this was consistently achieved, management wanted more significant results from its teams, such as innovation—something that was not being measured.

Management Styles and Practices

The third dimension of the cultural assessment is examining the management styles and practices that are prevalent at all levels, whether among senior managers, matrix managers, or project leaders. Leaders in a team culture need to be more facilitative and participative and create an open and trusting environment. They need to feel empowered themselves, to empower others, and to be willing to confront people and situations constructively.

You must find out what typical management styles are operating within the overall environment and the teams. Ask the following questions:

- ► Are you now managing teams in the same way you have always managed individual contributors?
- ► Do managers model teamwork among themselves and with their staff?
- ► What is different today from the past in how managers or team leaders manage?
- ► Which of your management practices have always supported teams and should continue?
- ► How does the management team encourage or discourage teamwork? What messages do the managers send by what they say, do, and reward?

The following examples illustrate a number of management style issues affecting the teaming culture.

► *Becoming more participative.* Mobil Oil's corporate security function was recently reorganized from a traditional hierarchical model to a flatter and leaner organization. It needed to transition from the former model to a more participative and consultative one, requiring greater teamwork than ever before with clients, staff, and contractors. The management team understood that the new culture required very different mind-sets and behaviors from what had been their norm, and they proactively requested assistance to make the change.

- *Managing in the old way.* IBM's Q&IT (Quality and Information Technology) organization reorganized into a new matrix structure. Many managers from the previous hierarchical structure became the team leaders in the new matrix. Although they no longer had direct control over team members, some continued to operate as the "manager" of their teams in the command-and-control mode, as if nothing had changed. They neither acknowledged the new requirements of the structure nor adjusted their style. This created issues that needed to be addressed in the Executive Direction phase.

- *Empowerment.* Just as traditional autocratic styles within a culture need to be addressed, so do management styles showing a lack of empowerment, as they can similarly block the success of teams. Five computer applications section heads in Mobil Oil's REEA (Research, Engineering, and Environmental Affairs) were tasked by their bosses to ensure improved coordination, communication, and delivery of service to their customers by becoming a steering committee for interdepartmental teams. The section heads were to speak with one voice in serving the client rather than the multiple and competitive voices that had been typical previously. In essence, they were asked to create a new subculture of teamwork. This was a major undertaking, given a history of conflict and competition among the five individuals and their departments. Moreover, they felt unempowered as individual leaders and did not operate as an empowered steering committee. They failed to make decisions or provide direction to their interdepartmental teams since they were unsure of their bosses' commitment or how permanent this subculture would be. So they deferred many decisions, and their teams had no direction and continued to operate in the old way. The steering committee members had to deal with their feelings of powerlessness and start making key decisions if they were to ensure a successful subculture. They dealt with this very positively and proactively during the Executive Direction retreat.

▸ *Avoiding confrontation.* A nonconfrontational, almost "polite" management style where no one was held accountable for results or change was interfering in the success of a newly merged chemical company. Following the merger, management did not inquire or monitor how the two original cultures were melding. Task forces were set up to deal with some issues, but management did not follow up to see if progress was being made. Many employees were paying lip service to the newly merged organization team without changing anything, and management did not confront them. There was a lot of conflict within the merged departments, but the managers simply tried to politely cajole people into harmony. The bottom line was that no one was being held accountable or felt accountable. This nonconfrontational style and deep-rooted politeness needed to be addressed within the culture to ensure the success of the new organization team.

These examples reinforce the importance of assessing management style and practices. The results of the assessment influence what needs to be addressed in the Executive Direction, subsequent events, and training.

Employee Styles and Behaviors

The fourth dimension of the cultural assessment examines employee styles and behaviors. It is important to understand how they correlate with the pervasive management philosophies and styles, and which ones work for and against the success of teams.

Employee styles are influenced by a combination of things. Certainly all of us have a proclivity toward a way of thinking and being, whether it be our level of confidence, whether we are individualistic or team-oriented, or what type of reactions we have to authority figures. Organizations often select individuals for those very characteristics, or sometimes in spite of them. The culture and prevalent management styles also mold the employee, who learns to respond, react, or cope in one way or another given the overall environment. A team culture requires that employees feel empowered—willing to speak up, identify problems, and share concerns as well as bring forth solutions. Employees need to be willing to initiate new ideas or projects and admit when something is not working. But empowered employees also must understand that empowerment has boundaries and doesn't always mean complete autonomy without any management direction.

Questions such as the following need to be posed to determine the prevailing employee styles:

- What are typical employee styles and behaviors?
- Are employees acting empowered?
- Are they fearful or cautious in what they say and do?
- Do employees feel valued?
- Do they actively contribute and share ideas, problems, and alternatives?
- Are they asking management for what they might need?
- Are they taking responsibility for their own behavior?
- Is "teamness" a natural feeling in the company, or have employees always operated as individual contributors? What is going on in the organization that might create these patterns of behavior?

The following examples depict different employee styles that can affect teamwork:

- *Fearfulness and lack of empowerment.* A serious example of passive, unempowered employees was a high-tech company whose past managers forced employees into a mind-set of extreme caution. A number of project teams felt strongly that their projects were a waste of resources and would not succeed in the end, but members refused to tell their new managers. When we asked why they didn't speak up, team members without exception looked at us incredulously and said, "No way are we about to tell them this isn't a good idea!" They were all going down a road they shouldn't have, dragging everyone and their resources with them, for fear of speaking up. Some other teams in the company weren't clear about the goals for their projects, but for fear of looking stupid they continued to work without asking for clarification. What is especially interesting about this organization is that the new management actively and consistently sought input on how things were going with the teams and whether the members had any concerns. Yet no one would speak up, since they were still operating in the old paradigm of cautiousness.

  ▸ *Too much empowerment.* An extreme contrast to the previous example is another company where employees felt so empowered that they would balk at any direction from management. Management guidance was interpreted as interference. Employees' reactions were so vehement that they ultimately intimidated management into not giving information and direction. The managers, who did not want to be perceived as autocratic or nonteam players, were concerned that they might have created monsters!

Employee styles impact the success of teams, so assessing this dimension and its implications about the culture is important.

Infrastructures (Systems/Policies/Procedures)

The fifth dimension of the cultural assessment is examining the infrastructures in place within the organization: the systems, policies, and procedures that exist that may promote or obstruct the team concept. The objective is to identify those needing to be modified or created. For instance, cultures that support teams require organizational systems that send the appropriate messages about the selection criteria for managers, employees, team leaders, and members. The criteria must reflect the new team-oriented requirements, as should rewards and performance management systems. In addition, communications systems for disseminating guidelines on how teams will operate should be in place.

  The following questions will help elicit this type of information on these systems.

  ▸ Who is currently in or being selected for leadership role? What messages do they give?
  ▸ Are people clear about what is expected of them in the team environment?

- How are employees being held accountable?
- Who and what are celebrated?
- How are people dealt with when they resist operating in teams or are dysfunctional?
- What procedures exist for how the teams will work?

The following examples show systems that supported the team construct or needed to be adjusted.

- *Policy statements stressing teamwork.* Positive statements in company policies about the importance and use of teams were prevalent at Attorneys' Title Insurance Fund. The Fund integrated such statements into its strategic plan and made them part of every employee's annual objectives. Contrast this with other organizations, where the word *teamwork* is never mentioned in the annual report or performance review.

- *Developing team procedures.* Rohm & Haas's Latin American division was initiating formal project teams for the first time but had no prescribed procedures for teams and needed to develop them. They needed procedures for how teams would get started, how teams would function within the normal day-to-day department operations, and what minimum requirements there would be for forming project teams—procedures that ultimately were developed.

- *Systems blocking teamwork.* In Mobil Oil's research and engineering departments, the accounting system was a major obstacle to the success of interdivisional teams. Until it was adjusted, the system inhibited the ability to share resources across divisions. It required a tremendous amount of red tape for resources to be shared, which discouraged the effort to do so.

- *The wrong rewards and celebrations.* One pharmaceutical company found that its reward-and-celebration system was inadvertently demotivating teams. When a drug was successful, the tradition was to celebrate the *entire* team, which consisted of many departments. But people felt that so many people were involved in the celebration that it diluted their feeling of being recognized. In addition, when a drug was not a winner, due to no fault of the teams, the organization tended to overlook acknowledging a great team effort. The reward and celebration system was corrected so that it no longer detracted from work.

These examples of how infrastructures can help or hinder the cultural support necessary for teams show why assessing this dimension of the culture is critical.

Level of Understanding and Agreement About the Team Concept

The sixth and final dimension of the cultural assessment is examining managers' and employees' understanding and agreement about the team concept. This establishes whether management has clearly defined and communicated the reasons for instituting teams. It also determines the level of understanding and agreement about those reasons among managers and employees. The results provide insights about potential education needs or pockets of resistance.

The following scenarios depict levels of understanding and agreement about teams.

▸ *Inadequate communication.* The reasons for moving to task forces were not clearly articulated in a utility company, because it was simply assumed employees would understand why, given the business environment. Management was using teams as a strategy to gain back a major loss in market share and to enhance morale, but most employees thought the move was a proactive step rather than to fix a problem. Management's hesitation to share its concerns about losing market share or poor morale made employees unaware of how serious the situation was and in turn reluctant to embrace the team concept.

A similar situation occurs in many health care organizations. They have moved to teams to address quality and to improve patient relations, with the underlying reason being survival. Yet there has been a hesitation to share that real reason with employees. Clearly defined reasons and expected outcomes are necessary in creating a supportive culture and motivated employees.

▸ *Varying levels of agreement.* The level of agreement people have with their company's reason for teams can vary among departments, sites, managers, or employees within the subcultures of an organization. In one part of a computer company, managers and employees understood why teams were instituted and felt that moving to teams was a long time in coming. However, they were uncertain as to how it was going to work. In other parts of the organization, managers understood the team idea but didn't really buy it, whereas employees were excited about the change. At yet another site, it was just the reverse, with management being extremely enthusiastic about the team concept while employees couldn't grasp why they needed to be a team. These differences within the various subcultures had to be reconciled.

The level of understanding and agreement about the team concept impacts the organization's success in implementing teams. Assessing this last dimension provides a baseline upon which to build activities for educating and dealing with resistance.

The six dimensions of the cultural assessment make up the first core element of the Needs Assessment. These dimensions help to isolate areas of strength to be reinforced and areas of weakness to be addressed. The next section looks at the second core element of the Needs Assessment: the team effectiveness assessment.

Team Effectiveness Assessment

The evaluation of team effectiveness examines two dimensions: (1) Focus In and (2) Focus Out, as illustrated in Exhibit 6-4. Focus In looks at the internal workings and processes of the teams. Focus Out looks at the external processes that teams use to interact with each other and work within the organization. The purpose of the assessment is to identify the team strengths and

Exhibit 6-4. The two dimensions of the team effectiveness
assessment.

---

1. Focus In: Internal Team Processes
2. Focus Out: External Team Processes

---

weaknesses that exist from both Focus In and Focus Out perspectives in order to determine relevant strategies in the culture
change.

Focus In

The Focus In dimension examines the internal team processes.
High-performance teams should have clear and agreed-upon
goals, roles, and norms for sharing information, resolving conflict, and making team decisions, to name a few.

Determining what works well with the teams and what
their typical frustrations and dysfunctions are tells a lot about
the awareness and skill levels of the team members, the procedures they institute, and the culture within which they operate.
It enables the teams to build on their strengths as it addresses
their weaknesses.

Some of the processes to evaluate include:

- How are team goals formulated and agreed to?
- How are team roles assigned?
- How are decisions typically made?
- How do team members share information?
- How are conflicts resolved or differences of opinions rec-
  onciled?
- How creative are team members in solving problems or
  achieving their goals?
- What leadership styles are prevalent?
- How do team members share responsibility?
- What norms or procedures have been agreed to among
  team members, with management, with the client, or with
  other teams?
- How do teams evaluate their own effectiveness?

These are the key processes for high-performing teams. The answers to these types of questions highlight what internal processes may help or hinder team effectiveness.

Here are a number of examples that show various internal team processes requiring attention.

▸ *Little contact among members.* In a data processing organization, most teams never met face-to-face even at the start-up of the teams, as a result of members' busy schedules and their being dispersed in separate geographic locations. Although they used e-mail, members complained about a lot of information falling through the cracks. Yet teams actually avoided meetings because they were perceived as unproductive, boring, and a waste of time, and many members preferred having minimal contact with other team members. The information-sharing issue had to be addressed, given its impact on the teams' effectiveness.

▸ *Decision-making problems.* In one health care organization, the team leaders made all the decisions because they were unable to manage differences of opinion among members. When the team members tried to make decisions, they did not confront conflicts that surfaced and made so many trade-offs under the guise of reaching consensus that their decisions were poor. Thus the team leaders would end up being the final arbiters. This pattern of decision making was counterproductive to the teams' success and needed to be dealt with.

▸ *Role Issues.* A real estate company experienced problems with the roles and utilization of team members. People were assigned roles based purely on their title or specialization, without discussion. Other team members' expertise and experience that might have been relevant to the assignment were never considered. In addition, in some instances there was duplication of effort as well as underutilization of talent. Teams contracted for technical expertise that actually existed within their own teams, but no one knew it. These role issues needed to be dealt with for the teams to be fully effective.

These are examples of some processes that can malfunction in teams. The goals of the Focus In assessment are to highlight the processes that work well and those that do not, the skills or procedures that need to be developed, and the challenges that the teams need to address. These issues are addressed in either the Executive Direction or training phases of the model.

Focus Out

The Focus Out dimension of the team effectiveness assessment examines the processes in place that teams and the organization use to interact with each other. It is here that we go beyond the parameters of the team and look at direction, communication, and interaction with the greater organization.

Well-thought-out procedures are needed to ensure that high-performance teams get what they need from the organization and vice versa. For example, a basic framework should be established and communicated about such things as:

- The selection process for team leaders and members
- Team project or goal initiation and flexibility
- Expectations for communication and feedback with management, other teams, and customers

The specifics of the procedures can vary. What is important is that the processes be established.

Inquiry about these procedures helps to identify any gaps that exist. Questions might include:

- How is the selection of team leaders and members managed by the broader organization?
- How does the organization create the team goals?
- What are the procedures or expectations for communicating with management, other teams, or the customer?
- What feedback loops exist?
- What accountabilities are defined?

The number and types of procedures in place vary from organization to organization. They might range from not having any procedures to assuming or expecting teams to develop the ones they need. The following examples illustrate that variation.

▸ *Setting goals.* Vague goals are sometimes handed to teams, with the expectation that they refine them as necessary—something that has worked well in some settings but not in others. In other situations, teams are provided with very specific, predetermined goals and parameters. The ability and comfort of teams to negotiate goals and the like determine the success of that procedure. If the company procedure for setting goals is infringing on the team's ability to achieve results, it needs to be addressed.

▸ *Prioritizing and communicating.* The need for management to establish mechanisms for prioritizing projects and communicating their status became clear at one of Gould Semiconductors' manufacturing plants. Management at the Idaho company had given the teams many project goals to achieve but had not prioritized the goals. The teams felt a little overwhelmed and were unsure of which to tackle first. In addition, there were no forums or ongoing reporting mechanisms in place at the plant where the teams could ask for input or provide status reports. This inhibited the teams from achieving the expected goals and was subsequently dealt with during the Executive Direction and training phases.

▸ *Procedural flexibility.* Teams in IBM's Q&IT were unaware of the flexibility they had for making changes in who were selected as team leaders and team members. Sometimes team leaders had the technical expertise but not the leadership skills necessary to facilitate the team, or team members did not have the appropriate technical skills. Sometimes too many people were assigned to teams, or for more time than was necessary. In all of these situations, the teams were unaware of what flexibility they had to make the appropriate changes. This procedural flexibility needed to be resolved in order for the teams to utilize their resources optimally.

▸ *Interorganization procedures.* Hamot Health Foundation, Alliance Health Network, and St. Vincent Health System—representing hospitals, long-term care, and home health care—formed an alliance to deal with the challenges of managed care within their community. The success of the venture (headquartered in Pennsylvania) was hindered by their distinct cultures, history of competition, and lack of agreed-upon procedures for interacting and formally operating. Senior management from all three entities needed to agree on some critical parameters within which to operate during the Executive Direction phase. Procedural issues needed to be dealt with at the operational level during subsequent phases.

Assessing Culture vs. Subculture

Whether you are attempting to change an overall culture or a subculture, the principles underlying the Needs Assessment generally stay the same. There is one exception, however. When you are attempting to change a subculture, you need to take into account the broader culture, which may place constraints on your degree of freedom and flexibility. Similarly, there may be positive factors within the overall culture that may promote change in and influence the subculture.

A classic example of a constraint is the performance management, bonus, and reward system, which is often standardized and imposed on subcultures. Yet even within those constraints, there are a number of things that managers can do informally to create their own adjustments to those systems. Once such issues have been identified as potential inhibitors to your team-oriented subculture, strategies can usually be developed to overcome them during the Executive Direction phase.

The positive factors within the larger culture also need to be capitalized on. For example, Bristol-Myers Squibb's senior team began espousing teamwork within the entire corporation, even developing and publishing a vision statement emphasizing teamwork. They also mandated team training. This was used by some departments as a reason and incentive to create more team-oriented subcultures.

Conducting the Needs Assessment

There are four phases in conducting the Needs Assessment process, as shown in Exhibit 6-5.

Exhibit 6-5. The four phases of the Needs Assessment process.

---

1. Preliminary Problem Definition
2. Data Collection
3. Analysis
4. Briefing the Results

Preliminary Problem Definition

The preliminary problem definition phase, which is the foundation for what follows, begins with an initial discussion, with the most senior manager of the culture or subculture being addressed. It could be the CEO, COO, general manager, vice-president, division head, or department manager (or a peer group of senior managers if they've been operating as a steering committee). It elicits his or her perspective and definition of the situation or problem at the time. This can vary from a description of symptoms, to an in-depth analysis, to a picture of the desired goals to be achieved by the new team culture. It might be problem-centered if problems are already occurring, or the need may be more proactive in planning the culture change to support teams. Expected outcomes from the culture change are preliminarily identified during this phase.

Data Collection

The data collection phase typically includes individual interviews with key people and interviews with focus groups. The focus groups usually include a representative sampling of organization members within the overall culture or subculture, ideally from varying levels, specialties, work units, and geographic locations.

The content of the interviews reflects questions about what helps and hinders team effectiveness as well as what in the culture works for or against teams. Sample questions might include:

- Why has the organization instituted teams?
- What is your greatest frustration with the team(s) you're involved in?

- ► What team successes can you name?
- ► What is management doing to support the team concept?
- ► What is management doing that is hindering the team concept?
- ► How does the corporate culture help and hinder teams?
- ► What would success look like, and what needs to be done to ensure that it occurs?

More targeted questions could be asked related to specific aspects of the culture. Surveys can be utilized as well to evaluate the culture and/or team effectiveness. For example, a survey on team effectiveness could evaluate how people perceive the current functioning of their team(s) according to key processes. A cultural audit could be used to evaluate the organizational values and norms against the requirements for a team culture.

A review of written documents is another element of the data collection process. This includes organization charts, strategic plans or annual reports, background statements on the team concept, vision and mission statements, and values or philosophy statements. Also, a review of various systems within the infrastructure is useful to assess any gaps or mixed messages. Some examples include the company's orientation program, performance management system and forms, reward system, and measurement system.

Actual observation of a sampling of team and/or management meetings is useful; it provides an opportunity to observe and take the pulse of team dynamics and cultural issues.

Analysis

The third phase is the analysis of the information gathered. An objective and clear view must be provided for the analysis to have impact. It should reflect patterns of issues rather than isolated instances or opinions. The ultimate summary should include an analysis of the key cultural issues that are helping and/or hindering teams. Team skills issues should be separated from systems issues.

Briefing the Results

The fourth phase is briefing the results. The briefing, prepared from the analysis just described, is given to the most senior individual within the culture or subculture being addressed—the person you first approached during the preliminary problem-definition phase. A synopsis of all issues and their implications is presented to the manager, who typically receives personal feedback along with coaching and consultation as part of the briefing. There may be some issues that only he or she can decide or take action on related to his/her own behavior or thinking, such as the fear that the manager may invoke in others or the manager's hesitancy to hold others accountable for follow-through. The manager may agree to deal with these and other issues in the upcoming Executive Direction retreat or in an individual coaching session.

The consultation and coaching of the senior manager also help to focus his or her thinking about vision for and expected outcomes from the organization's team concept, boundaries within which the senior team should work and make decisions for the Executive Direction at the retreat, constraints in determining the team construct and structure, and the culture change. There is negotiation on the next steps and the strategies to occur.

Although initially the briefing is conducted for the senior manager alone, all organization members receive data feedback during various planned events.

Exhibit 6-6 gives examples of findings that were included in briefings to various organizations.

Overview of Subsequent Events

As mentioned, the Needs Assessment phase stimulates a sequence of events to develop a plan for the culture change and to accomplish the required transition. The specific content, participants involved, and number and type of events vary, based on individual cultural or subcultural idiosyncrasies and the audit

Exhibit 6-6. Findings included in three organizations' briefings.

IBM's Q&IT

1. The senior team needed to reach full agreement about the team structure.
2. Policies and procedures needed to be developed to manage the team structure.
3. The workforce needed to be educated about the team structure and trained to work within it.
4. An orientation program needed to be developed to orient people who would join Q&IT in the future.
5. There were role-clarity issues that had to be dealt with.
6. The infrastructure systems needed to be examined to modify them to better support the team structure.

Attorneys' Title Insurance Fund

1. There was a loss of market share to competition from out of state.
2. Customer service needed improvement.
3. Customer satisfaction efforts were sporadic and uncoordinated.
4. Employees did not appreciate each other's roles or operate as an organization team.
5. The executive group was not in full agreement about the strategy to change culture.
6. Employees were not empowered to make decisions.

Mobil Oil REEA

1. There were historically discrete research and engineering departments with a history of competing and not working together.
2. There was a need to get customers involved in the process and improve partnerships.
3. There was a need to provide structure and clear direction for the new subculture.
4. Senior managers needed to empower themselves to make decisions and take action.
5. Systems needed to be adjusted to overcome inherent obstacles.

results. However, there are certain key events that do occur in all cases. These include:

- Executive or manager briefing
- Executive or management team retreats
- Work sessions for collateral teams
- Team retreats or training for the next level of management and intact teams
- Rollout events for the rest of the organization
- Follow-up events

The briefing, already described, is the first event. It ultimately clarifies and confirms the agenda for the upcoming executive or management team retreat, using the assessment results. The subsequent events are described in detail in the following chapters.

7

Using the Model: Executive Direction

Our plans miscarry because they have no aim. When a person does not know what harbor he is making for, no wind is the right wind.

—Seneca

The wisdom of the Roman statesman and philosopher Seneca leads us to the second essential step of the Change Model, which concerns actually defining what the culture or culture change will be and the how and why of the effort. We call this stage Executive Direction (highlighted in the overall model in Exhibit 7-1), because we firmly believe that an organization's culture emanates from the top. Each organization member may contribute to and mold its culture, but the boundaries, direction, and focus of the culture are determined by senior leadership. This stage immediately follows the Needs Assessment phase and uses the data uncovered there to determine how to proceed.

This chapter discusses why Executive Direction is important, describes its components, and provides information on conducting the Executive Direction retreat, at which important "products" are generated.

Exhibit 7-1. The Executive Direction phase of the Organization Culture Change Model.

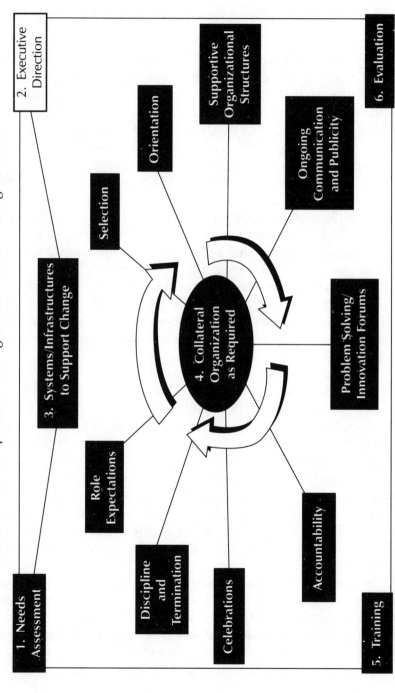

Why Executive Direction Is Important

When new organizations are formed as a start-up or through the likes of mergers, acquisitions, or alliances, it is senior leadership that must provide the definition, the impetus, and the planning for the new or modified culture. In fact, the Executive Direction set by the leaders becomes the driver for the organization's move forward to the new culture. Consider the following story.

There once was an organization that, because of a maturing product line and unforeseen competition from abroad, had to severely downsize its workforce. Soon after, the organization realized that it could not continue to survive doing work the way it always had. A wise senior executive convinced the leaders in the organization that formalizing work processes around teams, and no longer around a hierarchy, would greatly increase the efficiency and effectiveness of the workforce. Workers would use the skills for which they were hired much more than in the past, and the synergy gained from collaboration of workers would increase productivity and make the organization more competitive.

The organization leaders saw the wisdom in what the executive said, and they rushed out to their workforce and cried, "Teams! Teams! Teamwork! Teamwork!" The workforce tried very hard to please the leaders, but somehow the only results were confusion, frustration, and ultimately even lower productivity. They began to lose confidence in their leaders and to view the organization with distrust. After all, they were working longer, harder, and faster, but the leaders were never satisfied.

The leaders knew that the workers were able to work in teams; after all, they had been doing so, off and on, for years. So why were they rebelling, and why was the organization doing so poorly?

In this story (compiled from the real-life experiences of a number of organizations), the team concept from the executive was the correct one and the energy and motivation of the leaders and the workforce were admirable. However, as is often the case, though intentions are good, results don't follow. In our story, the organization needed to understand that the changes being requested constituted a real change in its culture and couldn't be treated as an ad hoc, minor correction to what had been done for years. As a major culture change, clear direction from the leaders was essential for success. For the workforce (and the leaders, for that matter) to rally and be successful in the change, the direction had to be clear and well communicated, with defined outcomes, clarified role expectations, a focused picture of the future, and a clearly articulated road map to get there.

Defining Executive Direction

Executive Direction is the process of ensuring that the senior leaders of an organization are all in concert regarding its culture toward teams. A senior team in this instance could be an executive team that reports to the CEO when dealing with an overall organization's culture, or it could be the management cadre of a department or division when dealing with a subculture within an organization. In a recent *Fortune* interview, GE's Jack Welch indicated that the mark of a good leader is his or her "ability to articulate a vision." This notion of articulating a road map (or vision) from where the organization is now to where it should eventually be regarding teamwork is the essence of this part of the Change Model.

Let's look at the following five aspects of Executive Direction:

1. Creating a unified perspective among the senior team about the new team culture
2. Defining what outcomes are expected from the new team culture
3. Getting a major commitment of resources and effort from everyone in the company
4. Ensuring that the members of the senior team understand and accept their role
5. Developing a plan for implementing the culture change

Creating a Unified Perspective

Executive Direction means creating a unified perspective among the senior team members about the new team culture. Organizations often undertake a major culture change assuming (or hoping) the senior leadership team is in agreement about the direction and degree of the change. But frequently this is not the case. When data from the senior team are analyzed, you may find that members have different concepts about teaming. Before you can lay out a unified perspective on the new team culture for the entire organization, you need to determine how the senior team feels about the following aspects:

- ► Will the entire organization participate?
- ► Will the new teaming construct be applied to everyone?
- ► To what degree is the senior team willing to restructure/ reorganize?
- ► Does the senior team fully understand, appreciate, and *agree* with the dramatic changes that may be necessary in changing from a traditional, hierarchical organization?

IBM's Quality and Information Technology organization was in the midst of a culture change to move from a hierarchy to a flatter horizontal organization composed solely of formal teams—a change being promoted by the vice-president. The senior team members were all advocates of teams and teamwork, but when pressed it was found that each had a very different perspective about the impending culture. Some shared the perspective of the vice-president that everyone in the organization would be operating in teams and that the hierarchy would cease to exist. Some agreed with the concept for only select parts of the existing organization (in other words, it was OK for the others, but not for their own part of the organization). And still others were against the teaming concept but were hesitant to share their feelings with the vice-president. Had Q&IT moved forward without first reconciling the views of the entire senior team, the culture change effort would have been doomed to an early failure. The unified perspective of the senior team, whether it be on a companywide culture change or an organizationwide subculture change, is essential for success.

Defining the Expected Outcomes

Another aspect of Executive Direction is clearly defining what outcomes are expected from the change to a new culture of teaming. These clearly articulated outcomes really answer two important questions:

1. What will the new teaming construct look like?
2. Why are we, as an organization, doing this?

Each person in the organization must understand what the new teaming construct will look like. When experiencing any change, a member of an organization must be able to see himself or herself as a part of the new order. If their various questions are answered clearly—such things as "Where do I fit?" "How will my role change?" "Whom will I be working with and for?" "What must I do differently?"—people will have an easier time supporting the change.

The question of why the organization is making this change is perhaps the most essential one needing to be answered to the satisfaction of all members of the organization if they are to support the change. Look at the following example.

Recently, a major division of a company in the energy business decided to move to a cross-functional teaming concept. As part of the Needs Assessment, members of the division were asked, "Why are we doing this?" Answers ranged from "I don't know" to "The division manager read an article in a magazine while flying back from a business trip" to "It's a clever way to get rid of some middle managers and employees." None of these answers even approached the real reason, which was to solve a problem of internal competition among computer sections in providing services to the same customer. Once the workforce was educated about the real reason, the culture change to cross-functional teams was heartily embraced.

Getting a Major Commitment

Often when contemplating a major change, the leaders of an organization do not truly realize what degree of commitment is necessary to ensure success. There is a tendency to believe that changing an organization's culture to a teaming concept is not really a big deal. But the change in organization culture needed to operate successfully in a teaming environment takes a major commitment of resources and effort, and so this is the third aspect of Executive Direction. It may take three to five years to realize the results and outcomes you've defined, and the time commitment for the senior team can be and usually is underestimated. In addition, managers and employees must be involved in planning and implementing the change, often as part of action teams and/or steering committees that guide the change. Changes in an organization's processes are often required, as are changes in the organizational structure and roles of employees and managers. All this means that a major commitment to training and orientation is a must.

Obviously, this major commitment must be clearly understood and agreed to by all of the leadership team if its members will be expected to support the change. The Executive Direction effort will ensure that agreement and understanding.

A major medical center had decided to make a major change to improve customer service through teamwork. The senior managers realized that merely training the employees would not accomplish what they wished to achieve. They decided to take on a culture change effort to ensure their success; on the surface, they were supportive. However, during their Executive Direction retreat, the senior managers realized the extent of the commitment that would be required to make the culture change, based on the data feedback. After some debate, they finally agreed to abandon the effort when they found that the level of commitment needed to expend the necessary resources (time, money, and people) was not there. They wisely decided not to attempt a major effort that would put their organization into turmoil, when the opportunity for success was so small and the opportunity for failure was so great.

Getting the Senior Team to Accept Its Role

Executive Direction also means ensuring that all members of the senior team understand the role required of them and agree to play that role. In too many instances, leaders feel that once they have initiated a change with a kickoff speech and a memo to all employees, the change will take place with no further emphasis from them. They fall into their old routines and continue with their traditional behaviors while expecting major change from everyone else. This behavior by the leadership team could spell disaster.

Senior leaders usually must make a very specific change in their roles to facilitate change in the rest of the organization. During an Executive Direction retreat, these specific roles are identified, discussed, and agreed to by all members of the team.

These roles usually fall into two categories:

1. Roles to facilitate and perpetuate the culture change
2. Roles that relate to the senior leaders themselves acting as a team

Some of the roles are shown in Exhibit 7-2.

Developing a Plan

Developing a plan for implementing the culture change is another part of Executive Direction. This plan must be specific only to the extent that everyone who will take part in the implementation clearly understands his or her role and what's expected of him or her. The plan is usually general in that it must recognize that the implementation is a long-term endeavor (typically three to five years) and must reflect the flexibility necessary for "course corrections."

The plan developed during the Executive Direction retreat identifies what form of collateral organization—if any—will be used (see Chapter 9) and dictates broad guidelines it will follow. These guidelines include reporting relationships, communications strategies, and monitoring mechanisms to ensure that the senior team is informed and up-to-date on progress and in-

Exhibit 7-2. Roles required of the senior team.

Roles in Culture Change	*Roles as Senior Team*
▸ Provide guidance/define direction	▸ Be a team
▸ Recognize and reward teamwork and team behavior	▸ Lead by example
	▸ Set common goals
▸ Monitor progress of culture change	▸ Share resources
	▸ Resolve conflicts constructively
▸ Communicate the new culture	▸ Make joint decisions
▸ Celebrate successes	▸ Be accountable
▸ Hold the organization accountable for expected changes	
▸ Address performance and behavioral issues	
▸ Provide resources/support	

volved at the appropriate times and places. In addition, the membership of the committees in the collateral organization is determined. Usually the names of those selected are published as part of the "products" from the Executive Direction retreat (discussed later in this chapter). Once the collateral organization begins its work, this general plan from the senior team becomes the basis for a more in-depth, detailed plan for implementation.

At Attorneys' Title Insurance Fund, the executive team's deliberations resulted in the creation of a collateral organization that consisted of an expanded executive team, a Steering Committee, and four action teams. The plan from the executive team to the Steering Committee consisted of a series of tasks that included such things as developing a kickoff campaign for the culture change, developing and communicating clear role expectations for employees regarding the new culture, developing reinforcement and feedback mechanisms, training the workforce on culture change and teaming, and developing accountability systems. The Steering Committee further defined the tasks and charged the action teams with completing the tasks and reporting status and requests for assistance back up the hierarchy. For example, the Steering Committee further defined the task of "developing reinforcement and feedback mechanisms" to be the revision of the annual performance review process and the company rewards-and-recognition system to support the new culture. The Steering Committee then assigned two of the action teams to make the revisions called for.

The plan for implementation from the senior team must also include what resources will be required and where those resources will come from. The team members must be clear about their expectation of how much time members of the collateral organization can and should spend on those duties in addition to their normal jobs. They must designate funding for the design, development, and delivery of training to ensure the culture change is successful.

Of primary importance, the senior team plan must address communicating the culture change and its implementation to all members of the organization. An effective initial and ongoing communications blitz that covers every aspect of the culture change is essential.

The Executive Direction Retreat

The major event in the Executive Direction phase is the Executive Direction retreat (called a go-away or off-site in some organizations). Through a facilitated, very efficient process, the retreat addresses whatever needs have surfaced in the Needs Assessment phase. The retreat tends to be an intense exchange of ideas, thoughts, concepts, and feelings among participants. Conflicts often arise that have to be dealt with and resolved, and decisions are made that dictate the future course of the organization and the careers of its members. This is not, perhaps, the more typical retreat where we play golf and build free time for a lot of social activities. It is an intense work session, often going into the late hours of the evening. The retreat provides a forum where it's OK to challenge direction and offer differing perspectives. It also provides the structure necessary to deal with issues effectively and constructively.

The event has two major purposes. One is to build the executive or senior leadership team around the new culture change toward teams. That means facilitating the senior leaders' agreement about what it is, what it looks like, what the outcomes should be, how to get there, who should be involved, what accountability should look like, and many other things. It also means having them act as a high-performing team that is a model for the rest of the organization. Team-building activities are used.

The second major purpose of the retreat is to generate the products described later in this chapter. These products are necessary to communicate expectations to the organization and are ultimately used as a catalyst for training the workforce.

We first discuss the logistics of the retreat, and then go on to the team-building activities used. This is followed by a discussion of how to conduct the event itself. A description of the products produced at the retreat concludes the chapter.

The Logistics of the Retreat

Who Should Participate?

In the belief that organization culture emanates from the top, we recommend restricting the Executive Direction retreat to the senior leadership team. For a companywide effort, that may include the president/CEO, the executive and/or senior vice-presidents who report directly to the CEO, and sometimes a deputy or special assistant who plays a key executive role. For example, when Attorneys' Title Insurance Fund embarked on a major companywide culture change, the Executive Direction retreat was attended by the president, the senior vice-president for operations, the senior vice-president for marketing, the senior vice-president for legal and administration, and the senior vice-president for finance—the cadre of senior leaders who are the decision makers and direction setters for that organization.

In the case of changing a subculture rather than the entire organization, the senior leadership team attends the retreat, that is, the senior person in the subculture and his or her direct reports as well. It may be a division director or department head, a branch chief and his or her section heads. In the case of a retreat involving the U.S. Food and Drug Administration's Office of Generic Drugs, the participants were the office director, his deputy, and the division heads of the reporting divisions. Three special assistants were also invited.

The point is, the participants are the very senior leaders who have the responsibility and accountability for the organization's performance. The usual number of participants ranges from five or six to ten or twelve.

How Long Should the Retreat Be?

Most Executive Direction retreats are scheduled for two or three days, depending in part on how far along the organization is in the culture change but primarily upon the results of the data gathering and analysis conducted during the Needs Assessment phase of the model. These data should indicate how well the senior team members usually work together, how they make decisions, and how far apart they are concerning critical decisions about direction, organization structure, procedures, support required, etc. Another consideration should be the experience the senior team has in working with a facilitator in a structured environment.

Some retreats go very smoothly, and working for two days from 8:30 A.M. to 5:00 P.M. is adequate to accomplish all the necessary tasks and exercises. However, every now and again the situation dictates a more intense and flexible effort. Take a recent retreat with a division of a large computer company that was implementing a formal teaming structure. There were differing opinions among the senior team regarding how much of the organization would be involved and what the final structure should be. Their planned two-day retreat ran for almost three days and went until after midnight on two nights! So plan to be flexible.

Where Should Retreats Be Conducted?

Retreats are usually held at some location away from the normal workplace. Obviously, this facilitates attendance, promptness, and attention from participants. When attempting a retreat in the normal workplace, the distractions of phone calls, secretaries, impromptu meetings, and drop-in customers or clients is difficult to overcome. Selecting a location where there can be refreshments, snacks, and catered meals in the work room gives you added flexibility and convenience when you need it most. Most retreats are held in hotels that cater to and understand business needs as opposed to family-oriented or vacation resort hotels.

When Should the Retreat Be Held?

The Executive Direction retreat should ideally be held very soon after the organization leader has been briefed on the results of the analysis of data gathered during the Needs Assessment phase. If possible and timing permits, any major decisions should be made at the retreat and not prior to it. Sometimes organizations attempt to implement teaming, and change is under way prior to a decision to treat the change as a *culture* change. In such an instance, the retreat should be held as soon as possible. The earlier that decisions can be made and agreements reached through the retreat, the easier it will be to alter any actions already taken.

How Are the Generated Products Handled?

Typically, the products generated at the retreat are captured on flip charts, as they are created through brainstorming and problem-solving sessions, facilitated discussions, and outright decisions. These flip charts are collected at the end of the retreat and typed in their raw form. A couple of volunteer participants then refine the raw data into presentable products that are finalized and sent to all participants for review and input. Once agreed upon, the final products are used in subsequent retreats or training sessions with the collateral organization and the workforce.

The Team-Building Model

A team-building model is typically used in actually conducting the retreat. Note that the Culture Change Model and its components form the content for the retreat, while the Team-Building Model provides the process or structure. The Team-Building Model described here and shown in Exhibit 7-3 has been used successfully with a number of senior leadership teams.

Exhibit 7-3. The Team-Building Model.

Focus In	Goals and Objectives	Focus Out
	Roles/Utilization of Resources	
L e a d e r s h i p T e a m	Control and Procedures (norms)	O r g a n i z a t i o n
	Problem Solving/ Decision Making	
	Trust/ Conflict Resolution	
	Communication	
	Experimentation/ Creativity	
	Leadership	
	Evaluation	

Each component of the model—used overall as the foundation for developing high-performance teams—is explored during the retreat through a variety of exercises tailored to address specific issues gleaned through the Needs Assessment process. These issues may relate to the senior team's interworkings (Focus In) or they may be specific issues the senior team needs to address in its relationship to the rest of the organization regarding the culture change (Focus Out). Team skills necessary to ensure successful team functioning are practiced as issues are resolved. Each Focus Out component results in a product for use in the culture change, which is then communicated to the organization as part of the Executive Direction and is used in subsequent activities with the collateral organization, intermediate levels of management, and workforce. Each Focus In component results in an action plan to ensure that the senior team members are held accountable for living up to their agreements as a high-performing team.

As the retreat unfolds, exercises are developed for each of the critical components of the model, designed to meet the needs and address the issues discovered in the Needs Assessment. Here's how that might play out:

Goals and Objectives

Focus In: Clear and agreed-upon team goals are necessary for high-performing teams. Participants work with existing team goals or develop new ones to help ensure a common team focus.

Focus Out: A philosophy is developed and a revised mission statement and/or vision statement is formulated if necessary. Organizationwide goals relating to teamwork are developed.

Roles/Utilization of Resources

Focus In: Specific team/team member roles are explored and clarified. The concept of effectively capitalizing on all available resources to address team issues is examined.

Focus Out: Roles for the senior team regarding supporting the culture change are generated. Input from the senior team regarding roles for the collateral organization and/or teams and team leaders is developed. Selection criteria may be developed for positions in the new culture or organization structure, for example steering committee member, action team member, team leader, etc. Expectations of employees in the new culture/environment are discussed.

Controls and Procedures

Focus In: Norms (rules) for behavior within the team environment are identified. The positive and negative impacts that these norms have on team members and the work environment are discussed. Action plans for developing improved norms and minimizing counterproductive norms are negotiated.

Focus Out: Guidance for specific procedures or constraints in the new culture are developed. Any spending or budget-related guidelines or time-accounting procedures are generated.

Problem Solving/Decision Making

Focus In: Participants examine their problem-solving and decision-making processes. A variety of alternative techniques are presented and applied in addressing current team issues and problems.

Focus Out: Guidelines for decision-making authority for teams at various levels are developed. Decisions regarding organization realignment or structure are made. Decision-making mechanisms during the culture change transition period are agreed upon.

Trust/Conflict Resolution

Focus In: The concept of and necessity for trust is explored. Particular skills and techniques for developing trust and resolving conflict are presented. An existing team conflict is addressed through the application of specific conflict resolution models.

Focus Out: In the new culture, methods for resolving conflict among teams, such as overlapping authority or responsibilities, must be worked out.

Communication

Focus In: Three aspects of high-performing team communications are examined: (1) interpersonal communication within and outside the team, (2) group dynamics as a team function, and (3) information sharing. These are discussed to help ensure optimal team results, and agreements are made.

Focus Out: Communication procedures throughout the new culture and organization are identified. Reporting requirements of teams to their customers/clients and to the senior team are developed. Sharing of information across teams is emphasized and methods to do so are developed.

Experimentation/Creativity

Focus In: High-performing teams require explicit mechanisms to focus the creative energy of team members. Techniques are provided and utilized to bring innovative solutions to actual team issues.

Focus Out: Empowerment of teams is discussed and the degree of team self-sufficiency and participation is decided.

Leadership

Focus In: The concept of shared leadership and power is discussed. Specific leadership roles are pinpointed that should be thought of as shared roles to enhance team performance. Various aspects of power are presented to provide the catalyst for teams to assume accountability for their own power.

Focus Out: Team leadership criteria and requirements are agreed to. People are selected for leadership roles for teams and for the collateral organization according to the criteria.

Evaluation

Focus In: Teams typically evaluate results. An additional focus is provided on the evaluation of team process. The importance of the *how* in team performance is stressed. Actual team dynamics are observed and feedback is used to develop action plans for improvement.

Focus Out: Standards for Success are developed as a benchmark to assess the progress and success of the new culture and the transition to the new culture.

Conducting the Retreat

Following some general introductory activities (such as introductions, an icebreaker, establishing norms, and sharing the retreat goals and agenda), the retreat really begins with a briefing to the participants in which the results of the Needs Assessment are presented and discussed. This ensures that everyone agrees with the data and the recommendations and that the agenda and topics of the retreat are tied directly to the real issues and concerns of the organization regarding culture and teaming.

The next step in the agenda is to educate the senior team participants about changing the culture toward teaming and, more specifically, about the Organization Culture Change Model. Each aspect of the model is thoroughly explained and the participants are shown the importance of creating this new culture as a strategy to successfully implement the formalized team concept. This exercise is very important, for it is here that the senior team members must be in agreement about culture change as a strategy and about their commitment as individuals, a team, and an organization to stay the course. As an example, frequently there is a lot of discussion and sometimes difficulty in agreeing on a common stand about accountability or discipline and termination. Once there is understanding and agreement, we then move to the team-building model as a structure for the remainder of the retreat. Here are some examples of how exercises were used to arrive at action plans and products.

▸ *Conflict resolution.* The executive team of IBM's Q&IT organization was not in agreement about the organizational structure or who in the organization would participate in the new teaming structure. It was imperative that this issue be resolved early on, before any other products could be developed. Thus, the first component of the Team-Building Model to be addressed was conflict resolution. The Focus In aspect was used to give the team members the conflict-resolution skills they needed. The participants in the exercise were made aware of their styles and propensities in resolving conflict. Then they learned about methods to resolve conflict. For their action plan, they agreed on a process to communicate, address issues, and arrive at norms of behavior as a team.

Now, as part of Focus Out, the team was ready to address the issue of organization structure. The exercise began with the presentation of three different structures for teaming that could be used. The senior team was divided into three subgroups, with each given one of the structures, and told to develop a list of pros and cons as that structure related to their organization. Each subgroup reported its results to the entire team. The team was then facilitated through a discussion of why the organization was entertaining the idea of a formal team structure at all, a discussion that confirmed the need and the original idea. The pros-and-cons exercise made it obvious to everyone which structure would accomplish what they needed—this was the Focus Out product—and the decision and their commitment allowed the team to move forward.

▸ *Communication.* The Latin American division of Rohm & Haas, an international chemical company, was trying to introduce a teaming concept to address quality issues in its operation. The senior leadership team members saw their areas as so separate and distinct that they rarely communicated. In fact, their heavy travel schedules and those of their subordinates exacerbated the lack of communication. Under the aegis of Focus In in the communication component of the Team-Building Model, they addressed the quality issues and finally agreed that to solve them as teams, there was a real need for the senior team (1) to begin regularly communicating with each other, and (2) to begin to act as a Latin American management team rather than in separate silos as had been their norm. The action plan was thus to discuss quality and to all be in the office one day each month to meet. Then, in the Focus Out part, one aspect of the product was the establishment of expectations and procedures for the entire office to arrange travel schedules and calendars so that everyone—not just the senior team—would be in the office the same day each month. That day was set aside for an all-hands meeting and for quality teams to meet to address issues. These procedures and expectations were communicated to the entire office as part of the Executive Direction for the culture change.

▸ *Leadership.* The Biostatistics and Data Management Department of Bristol-Myers Squibb had just hired a new department manager. She realized that the two divisions in the department were completely independent, and that the subordinate managers were deferring entirely to her and were not sharing leadership responsibilities for operations. During the Focus In part of the leadership component, the executive team made agreements to begin to interact more. They accepted responsibility and created action plans to ensure that they would begin to share leadership responsibility with the new department head.

▸ *Controls and procedures.* In the Focus Out session under controls and procedures, this same Bristol-Myers Squibb team dealt with a problem regarding how the two divisions interfaced from the start of a project to its conclusion. The team laid the groundwork for what eventually became a thirty-step process to ensure greater interaction, collaboration, and communication.

Once all the products and action plans are produced, the retreat closes with an exercise to develop a high-level implementation plan for the culture change that serves as a basis for further, more detailed plans later during the change effort.

The Executive Retreat Products

The products generated at the executive retreat are finalized and published soon after, to be used by the collateral organization members for guidance. (The collateral organizations often expand upon them as well.) The products are used as base materials in subsequent training and team-building activities. The products may include such things as:

▸ *Revised mission statement and/or vision statement.* The revised mission statement describes the new way in which work gets accomplished through teams. The revised vision statement describes the target picture of the organization in its new teaming environment, once the culture change has been accomplished.

▸ *A philosophy.* This statement of philosophy serves as a vehicle to inform the organization about what the leadership feels regarding the new teaming environment it is advocating. It serves as a guideline for decision making and action. Exhibit 7-4 is the philosophy for teams that the senior management team of IBM Q&IT devised at its Executive Direction retreat.

Exhibit 7-4. The team philosophy product produced at IBM's Q&IT retreat.

Team Philosophy
▸ We will accomplish our mission through TEAMWORK!
▸ We believe teaming is a basic skill critical to our success and it is the fundamental operating principle through which we satisfy our customers, develop our skills, and deliver world-class results.
▸ Each of us, through our team affiliations, has the responsibility to establish customer expectations (really know our customers) and the power to fulfill those expectations.
▸ We take pride in our organization and strive for excellence, differentiating ourselves through our enthusiasm, creativity, responsiveness, and trust in one another.
▸ We encourage having fun—it's contagious and contributes to the team's creativity and success.
▸ Our identity is our ability to combine our talents through highly effective and committed teams to delight our customers—accepting their problems as our own.

▸ *Executive management and employee roles.* The senior team members sometimes generate a list of roles that they expect managers, employees, and themselves to learn and practice in a new culture of teaming and teamwork. Exhibit 7-5 reflects the roles of the Manufacturing Team that guided Mobil Oil's science and technology focus team effort within the Research, Engineering, and Environmental Affairs (REEA) and Marketing and Refining (M&R) technology management function. The Manufacturing Team generated and committed to these roles at its Executive Direction team-building session.

▸ *Standards for Success.* The Standards for Success are measurements that the senior team and the rest of the organization can look at to monitor the road to success. The standards typically include measurements that relate to the reason why the organization has undertaken this culture change. Exhibit 7-6 is the result of the efforts of the executive team from Attorneys' Title Insurance Fund to clarify what the company would measure as success indicators for its culture change.

▸ *Decisions about and descriptions of new organizational structures.* New structures are often required when changing a culture toward teaming. This product provides descriptions of these new structures: matrix organizations; flatter, more horizontal organizations with a much reduced management hierarchy; condensed departments formed from several original departments; more formal cross-functional/cross-organiza-

Exhibit 7-5. The manufacturing-team roles product produced at Mobil team-building workshop.

Manufacturing Team Role
▸ Provide leadership and direction.
▸ Encourage prudent risk taking.
▸ Evaluate and reward success.
▸ Remove obstacles to S&T (science and technology) success.
▸ Sell the program within and outside the organization.
▸ Balance client needs with capability to implement.
▸ Ensure commitment and participation of our direct reports.

Exhibit 7-6. The Standards for Success product produced at the Attorneys' Title Insurance Fund retreat.

Standards for Success

- ▸ Increase in market share
- ▸ Improvement in turnaround time
- ▸ Increase in customer satisfaction (internal and external)
- ▸ Decrease in number of complaints
- ▸ Increase in number of compliments/comments
- ▸ Meet certification dates
- ▸ Decrease in turnover
- ▸ Increase in number of new customers (external) and bringing back defectors
- ▸ Increase in business with existing customers
- ▸ Decrease in error rates
- ▸ Customer service performance appraisal ratings
- ▸ Customer service award systems

---

tional teams; competency centers; global or joint business areas; core and extended project teams; etc.

▸ *Specific work process procedures/guidelines.* Senior teams frequently develop and impose very specific procedures and/or guidelines to ensure that expected outcomes are met efficiently and effectively. These guidelines may deal with topics such as reporting information, documenting processes, communicating upstream and downstream, project monitoring, and spending and accounting procedures. Exhibit 7-7 is an example of a review process that was developed and agreed to by the Mobil Oil Manufacturing Team to review the technology management function planning process.

Once these executive retreat products are rolled out to the organization, they become the heart and the drivers for the culture change effort.

Exhibit 7-7. The annual-review-process product produced at Mobil team-building workshop.

Annual Review Process

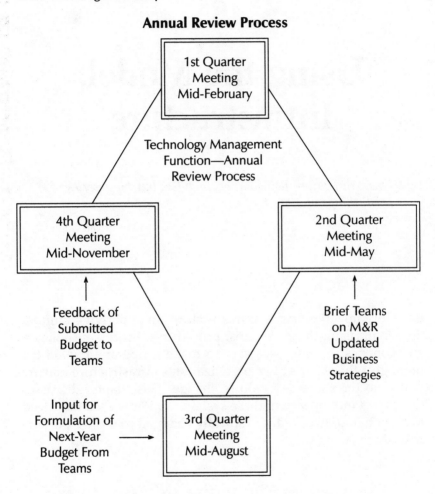

8

Using the Model: Infrastructure

Great things are not done by impulse, but by a series of small things brought together.

—Vincent van Gogh

Every organization has an infrastructure: an underlying foundation comprising those systems, procedures, processes, policies, and controls that are necessary to make it operate. Exhibit 8-1 highlights those parts of an organization's infrastructure that are critical to the success of culture change. This chapter discusses the importance of each of these systems and how each may need to be initiated, tweaked, or radically changed to ensure the success of the change.

The Need for Supportive Infrastructures

Once an organization has decided to make a change to a more team-oriented environment, the Needs Assessment has identified what issues need to be addressed, and the senior management team has provided its Executive Direction, the next step is to begin to set up systems that clarify, reinforce, and reward expected behavior in support of the culture change and teams. Changing these systems sends a clear message to the organiza-

Exhibit 8-1. The Infrastructure Components of the Organization Culture Change Model.

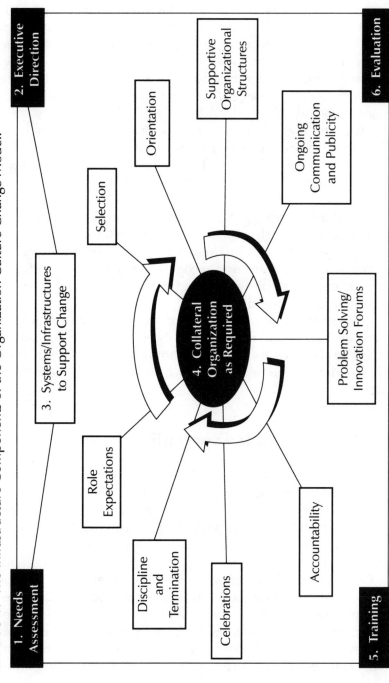

tion that this change is for real and that the organization is serious. Once made, the changes not only prepare the organization for its new environment but also formalize and document the changes in a way that provides an orientation to the new culture. This documentation becomes useful during training for people affected by the change as well as orientation for new employees coming on board.

Changing these systems is no easy feat since they are typically ingrained and deep-rooted. But without these supportive systems, the move to teams will be short-lived, just another fad.

Infrastructure systems are found in both an overall organization culture and in its subcultures. When attempting to modify the infrastructure of a subculture, be aware of and pay attention to any infrastructures imposed from the overall organization. For example, when tweaking (modifying) what behaviors you want to reward and recognize in the new subculture, you must consider policies dictated in the reward-and-recognition system of the overall company.

This chapter dissects each part of the infrastructure and discusses what an organization should be trying to accomplish by creating or changing its systems. Examples are used to illustrate ways in which some organizations have dealt with their infrastructure.

Role Expectations

We believe that people want to do right by their organizations. People want to succeed personally, and they want their organizations to succeed. Certainly a way to help people achieve this success is to educate them about what is expected. If they truly understand this, they will strive to meet and even exceed those expectations.

Organizations have many ways to educate employees about what is expected. Some have formal job descriptions that break each job down into components and explain in detail the requirements to be successful. Some have job aids, which are tools typically used to train people in their job requirements. More often, managers and supervisors share their expectations through one-on-one meetings with subordinates. These meetings may be very formal, or as informal as a boss making a short comment to an employee. Regardless of how the expectations get shared, the important point is to share them in a clear, concise, straightforward way.

When organizations are engaging in a culture change toward teams, it is obvious that what is expected of people in the organization also changes. Managers must manage differently. They must become more collaborative, they must delegate more, they must empower the worker, and they must reward and evaluate new behaviors. Employees must also behave differently. They must be more collaborative, they must share information with more people, they must communicate across traditional boundaries, and they must take on more responsibility and become real team players.

In a team environment, boundaries become fuzzier, structure becomes more nebulous. The safety net of hierarchy is lost. Traditional comfort zones are erased. Everyone in the organization is affected by the change. In order for people to get past the trauma of change, they must be able to know that they are valuable employees who are contributing to the organization. Stimulating that contribution should begin with a clear articulation of what the organization expects of them.

This articulation of expectations can take many forms. For example, as part of a major culture change, the newsroom of the *Fort Lauderdale Sun-Sentinel* established new expectations of all managers and supervisors regarding decision making. To clearly communicate the new expectations, the senior management group developed a decision-making matrix (Exhibit 8-2) that described the new responsibilities at each level for making decisions regarding travel, the budget, hiring, etc.

The newsroom also found that messages from the vice-president/editor were often being misinterpreted by the staff. This led to "Unmixing Mixed Messages" (Exhibit 8-3), a product communicated throughout the newsroom as part of the culture change.

As a result of a culture change, the roles of organization members may be expanded or diminished, and very often new ones are created. The creation of new roles or the modification

Exhibit 8-2. The decision-making matrix at the *Fort Lauderdale Sun-Sentinel.*

Decision Categories			Who		
	Editor	Managing Editor	Senior Editors	Dept. Heads	Assistant Dept. Heads
News Exceptions: Special additions/sections, breaking format, or house stories require editor in chief's and managing editor's approval.					X
Budget Exceptions: ➤ Every level must follow the imposed spending limits. ➤ Payroll changes, transfer between accounts lie with editor in chief/managing editor. ➤ Exceeding the budget calls for approval at the senior editor level. ➤ Contingencies approved by department heads.				X	

Personnel
Exceptions:
➤ Hiring. Department heads with input from asst. department heads.
  (Editor/managing editor approve hires of personnel at the dept. head level or above.)
➤ Formal discipline lie with the senior editor group.
➤ Firing/suspensions lie with the managing editor.
➤ Salaries outside the standard grid approved by editor in chief.
➤ Co-signing loans approved by managing editor.
➤ Changing beats of reporters lies with the assistant dept. head
  unless it crosses areas; then it lies with the department head.
				X	

Legal/Ethical/Political Major considerations must be the integrity of the newspaper and liability against the newspaper. Editor/managing editor are the decision makers.	X	X			
Long-Term Projects Projects that cross organization lines and/or expend extraordinary resources.			X		
Travel Exceptions: ➤ Travel to a hostile environment approved by editor. ➤ Travel in conjunction with training; coordination must be with training editor.				X	
New Ideas/Suggestions for Change	X	X			

© 1989 Corporate Management Developers, Inc.

Exhibit 8-3. "Unmixing Mixed Messages" at the *Fort Lauderdale Sun-Sentinel.*

Unmixing Mixed Messages

▸ "Keep me informed!"

The real message is, tell me what you've done, not what you want to do.

▸ "Do the right thing."

The real message is, doing the right thing is *not* what I want. Doing the right thing means that when you consider decisions, consider factors such as fairness, necessity, the priority, the timing, and the discipline and praise that go along with decision making. It also means not abdicating your role as a decision maker.

▸ "Do something, make a decision."

The real message is, taking considered action is better than taking no action at all.

▸ "Keep the reader in mind."

The real message is, this paper is for the reader, not for *us!*

▸ "We've always done it this way." (from a plaque on the wall of the VP/editor)

The real message is,

---

of existing ones is linked directly to the new culture and team environment and the behaviors that will ensure that the change is successful. Unless new behaviors are demonstrated, the old way of doing business will never be eliminated and the new way never implemented.

The following are some examples of how role expectations were changed in organizations undergoing a culture change toward teams.

▸ *Describing a specific role.* In IBM's Q&IT, nearly all roles in the organization changed when it moved to a teaming environment using a matrix configuration. During the Executive Direction retreat, the management team defined its own role in the new culture as well as the roles for the next level down in the organization. These latter roles described new positions that operated in an entirely different way. These roles, as described by the management team, were then refined by the newly selected incumbents. The final roles product was then published along with other products generated during the Executive Direction phase. Exhibit 8-4 shows how the roles of Business Area Leaders (at the next level down) were defined.

▶ *Revising job descriptions.* The senior management group at Attorneys' Title Insurance Fund assigned a task to an action team to revise the formal job descriptions for every position in the company. Revisions and additions to the job descriptions included very specific behaviors that the Fund felt were critical to the success of its culture change. Although this was a gargantuan task, the result was that each incumbent and new employee was aware of the specific behaviors required to be successful.

The products generated when an organization deals with role expectations are essential in changing employee behavior and should be developed as a first step in dealing with the infrastructure. They become the basis for many of the other steps. For example, the modified roles and behaviors become the basis for the annual performance management system used to hold people accountable for change. They also help to define the criteria for selection and promotion and form the basis for changing the awards and recognition systems.

Selection

In moving toward an environment of formal teaming, an organization must begin to think differently when making decisions about hiring new employees and managers, selecting people to fill specific positions (e.g., team leaders, task force members, or matrix managers), and promoting people into leadership positions. Traditionally, these decisions were made using criteria that relied heavily on technical competence. Sometimes other

Exhibit 8-4. Business Area Leaders' roles at IBM's Q&IT.

Business Area Leaders' Roles

- ► Define strategic direction and goals for the business area.
- ► Define mission and goals for each business area program.
- ► Manage the business area project portfolio.
- ► Monitor business area programs (execution, measurements, tracking, and budget controls).
- ► Coordinate total effort for a business area.
- ► Define objectives and visions for work activity within the program.
- ► Coordinate total work effort for a program.
- ► Drive business solutions from conception to completion.
- ► Identify opportunities within a given focus area.
- ► Provide input to the operations and budget planning processes.
- ► Interface at executive levels.
- ► Interface with multiple organizations.
- ► Maintain morale of teams working on program activities.
- ► Establish prioritization of skill needs across Q&IT.
- ► Participate in project portfolio prioritization process.
- ► Identify and prioritize resource requirements by project and provide to the competency center management team.
- ► Provide appraisal input to Competency Center Managers.
- ► Participate in establishing team objectives, goals, milestones for measures of success, recognition incentives (financial), and celebrations.
- ► Demonstrate a commitment to teamwork.
- ► Act as a "coach" to project teams.
- ► Attend competency center meetings to facilitate teamwork and communication.
- ► Interlock performance plan with project plan with Competency Center Manager and employee.
- ► Ensure that teamwork and skill development requests are clearly defined for Competency Center Managers by employee assigned to team.
- ► Negotiate upward based on workload and skill availability.
- ► Contribute to and participate in strategic business planning (focus on culture change and project goals).

criteria were considered, such as longevity, political connections, or friendships. But if your culture change is to be successful, the list of criteria must change. In addition to relying on technical competence, a new criterion of *compatibility* with the new culture must play an equally important part.

This notion of compatibility sends a strong message throughout the organization that change is indeed under way. It clearly articulates what attributes are important in the new culture; by selecting people with these attributes, we help to ensure that the organization will be successful in that new culture.

To meet the compatibility objective in the selection process, our hiring, selection, and promotion decisions must reflect the new team and role expectations. To ensure compatibility, the criteria must be specific in describing the attributes and behaviors expected from those selected.

Selection decisions are guided by the selection system (part of the infrastructure). There may be a variety of selection systems in place such as a recruitment system, a hiring system, a probationary system for new hires, a promotion system, and a system for selecting people as team leaders or team members.

There are many methods that may have to be tweaked within these systems. For example, you may need to change the wording in media advertisements and internal job postings to reflect new expectations. Job applications should be changed to ask specifically about experience on teams or past positions that required the behavior you now expect. Many companies have a set of standardized job interview questions that can be changed to help managers probe potential new employees about their experience in working in and with teams. The questions may also explore a candidate's comfort and ability to interact and communicate with others, whether he or she prefers to work alone or with others, or how adaptable and flexible he or she may be.

Here are a number of examples from organizations that have changed their infrastructures with regard to selection processes.

▸ *New selection criteria.* Mobil Oil's Mobil Technology Company (MTC) recently changed its culture to one emphasizing teamwork and partnerships with both internal and external "partners." This partnering required different leadership skills than Mobil had previously required. To choose the leadership for the new organization, a leadership selection process was developed and implemented involving 360-degree input about candidates. The criteria developed for selection and about which data were gathered in the 360-degree process were having a clear vision and bold strategies, being an effective communicator, being concerned for results, valuing people, and being committed to technology. Using these criteria, MTC selected leaders at every level who were not only competent but compatible with the new culture.

▸ *Change in advertising.* Attorneys' Title Insurance Fund now includes in all job advertisements and internal job postings the requirement that applicants possess excellent interpersonal (team) and customer service skills. The company has also revised its job application form to require input upon which to assess the compatibility question.

▸ *Desired characteristics.* IBM's Q&IT organization has begun publishing guidelines for employees working in its matrix-managed organization. Under a section of the guidelines titled "Organization Staffing," it says: "In seeking new staff for Q&IT, resource managers should consider how well candidates will work within the organizational framework in addition to evaluating their skills, technical expertise, and business knowledge. To be successful in the Q&IT environment, an individual must be adaptable, must have good interpersonal skills, and must be a good team player." The guidelines go on to list detailed characteristics that can be used by anyone conducting interviews or reviewing resumes.

Orientation

As a part of any team culture change, it is critical that all members of an organization be oriented to the new culture, what the organization has done and is doing to create a supportive environment for teams, and what contribution is expected of them. Viable orientation programs can be updated to include the critical aspects of the culture change. If there is no orientation program, a mechanism must be created. In either case, both current and future employees must go through the orientation program.

The orientation should include, at a minimum, relevant products produced during the Executive Direction phase, any products or policies generated or revised during the Infrastructure phase, and any description of any organizational structures (such as an organization chart). The products may include such things as the organization vision/mission statement(s), a discussion about new or revised role expectations, a philosophy and reason for the new culture, any current implementation plans, and a retrospective look at what the organization has done to change the culture thus far.

There are various methods for delivering an orientation program. It may be through a rollout of training programs to prepare people for the new culture, it may be through a formal human resources orientation program, it may be a video presentation sent to remote sites, or it may be a manual or pamphlet distributed to employees. The most effective programs seem to be those that include contact with senior organization leaders. The ability to ask questions, clarify concepts, and address concerns directly to someone "in the know" goes a long way in increasing receptivity to the culture change.

When Mobil Oil, in its REEA organization, instituted what it called CADET (computer application development) teams and later science and technology focus teams, a short manual was produced and distributed to team participants. This orientation manual contained goals of the programs, roles of the various players, specific procedures to be followed, Standards for Success, and measurements to be tracked and monitored. The CADET and focus teams met with a panel of four organization leaders, who addressed issues, clarified procedures, and answered questions. The panel also demonstrated the unity and cohesiveness of the organization leaders.

At Saturn, a two-day orientation program addressing what it calls "yesterday and tomorrow" is being used to educate and unify 5,500 employees about past, present, and future hurdles and the "why and who" of what's happening in the company.

Sears recently replaced a 29,000-page manual of policies and procedures with a simple folder (titled "Freedoms and Obligations") which tells managers what they are responsible for and what freedom they have to make decisions; it also provides a code of business conduct for all employees.[1]

These procedures are examples of how organizations can be successful in their attempts to orient the workforce about change.

Supportive Organizational Structures

Assume for a moment that every organization is ideally structured in a way that facilitates how work is accomplished. Then assume that our organization decides to move to formalized teams. Can we again make an assumption that the organization will change its structure to facilitate teaming? Definitely not! Organizations tend to shy away from major changes in structure, even though their culture is changing. This failure to move to a supportive organizational structure is one reason why organizations fail in their desire to work more in a team environment.

As you move toward teaming, you must be willing to address the obstacles in your current structure and work process that can thwart a team culture and the ultimate success of teams.

One aspect that almost always presents an obstacle to formal teaming is the typically very rigid hierarchical structure many organizations are used to. In such a hierarchy, managers tend to hold on to their people tenaciously, even using the terms *my people* or the folks *I own*. Although these command-and-control managers do allow participation in some teams, they can't cope with the flexibility and fluidity demanded by the new teaming culture. In addition, typical hierarchical structures usually have an autocratic management style, with lots of layers of departments, divisions, branches, and sections operating as individual silos. These silos frequently are competing for resources and customers and thus seldom share information or resources. (We also sometimes find silos of one person or a few people within the same organization function that, due to current structures and processes, are competing or at least not collaborating. These smaller, individual silos can be as inhibiting as the larger organizational ones.)

The task in this part of the model is to create a new structure (or structures) that supports and facilitates the teaming concept. These new structures and/or procedures should result in mechanisms that break down the walls or lay down the silos such that it is easy and natural to work in teams and to collaborate rather than compete. The mechanisms can be as formal as reorganizing into a matrix or as informal as arranging time in schedules for teams to meet. They could be as formal as altering accounting systems to allow for the easier transfer of resources or changing compensation systems from ones that promote competition (typical in sales organizations) to ones that encourage collaboration and teamwork; they could be as informal as sponsoring a cross-division bowling or golf team.

Supportive structures could include a flatter organization with less hierarchy and more autonomy; a standing cross-functional team whose charter is to solve large issues across the organization; a formal process to facilitate the forming of quick reaction, short-term teams; or training courses open to all who feel they need skills to work in teams.

One example of a supportive organizational structure was set up in late 1995 at General Motors. A number of vehicle line executives were named to lead teams that would manage the product development process for a vehicle line, such as small cars. These teams are vested with the authority to make decisions governing design, engineering, manufacturing, marketing, quality, etc., which previously were spread over the GM hierarchy. This move to a new structure supports the team concept at GM and decreases the time it takes to develop new vehicle lines and reduces the corporate infighting that has historically occurred.

Exhibit 8-5 shows another supportive organizational structure, the matrix set up at IBM's Q&IT. All workers have been assigned to competency centers that report to the human resources department. Project teams are formed across the competency centers to accomplish the work required for each of the

Exhibit 8-5. The organizational matrix at IBM's Q&IT.

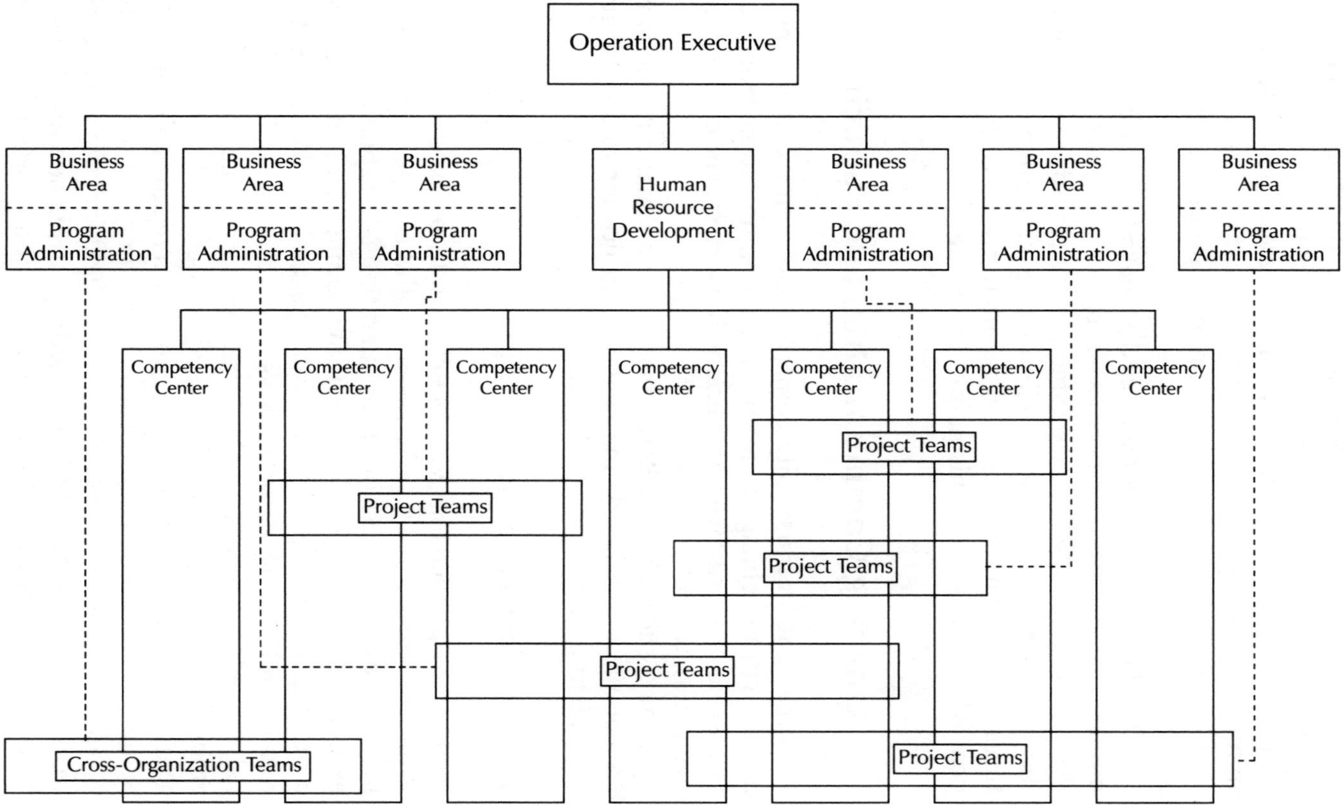

business areas. The matrix replaces the traditional hierarchy where project work was done within departments or sections and not in fluid teams across the organization. This reduced the number of managers and created opportunities for employees to use their skills on a variety of projects throughout the organization.

The nonsupportive structures that may currently be in place and the need for new supportive structures are typically discovered through the Needs Assessment process. Addressing these discoveries by modifying or eliminating nonsupportive structures and creating new ones to facilitate teams is the ultimate goal when considering this part of the model.

Ongoing Communication and Publicity

An organization must fully communicate with its constituents about a culture change to teams. The communication cannot be of the one-dose, single-event variety. If ever a situation called for overcommunicating, this is it.

Since such drastic alterations are being made in the way the company does work, massive communication and publicity become imperative.

What to Communicate

Begin with publicizing why the change to teams is necessary. What problem is being addressed? Is the change primarily to increase responsiveness or turnaround time? To capitalize on the expected synergy to be derived from teaming? Or is it to realize a more effective use of critical but scarce skills? Whatever the reason, publicizing it to employees, customers, and suppliers helps them understand the logic behind the change and thereby embrace it. The products we've discussed so far should be shared. The philosophy of the organization regarding teams, the Standards for Success against which the company will measure progress, and the new role expectations held for employees now working in teams must all be effectively explained and the explanation communicated and publicized. If any new policies or procedures have been initiated or existing ones modified, they too must be publicized and explained in depth.

Key positions in the teaming construct and the names of people selected to fill those positions must be communicated. A new organization chart or functions diagram explaining any changes in the structure must be quickly developed and sent to everyone. This chart must be kept up to date to reflect the evaluation of the culture change, and these periodic updates must again be sent to every interested party. If other structural elements are changed, they must likewise be publicized and communicated. These structural elements include such things as telephone number changes; different mailing addresses; new position titles; and new forms, formats, and methods. Progress in the culture change should be communicated as well. In short, anything that is different as a result of the culture change should be publicized and communicated.

How to Communicate

A key here is the need for ongoing communication and publicity. Customers and suppliers, but especially employees, must be kept constantly up to date on the culture change as it evolves.

Many organizations find that at the outset of a culture change, a kickoff event or ceremony is an effective way to get the word out. This event is normally conducted by the senior leader in the organization (the CEO or president of a company for an overall culture change, or the vice-president, director, or unit chief for a change in a subculture). This kickoff event should be well orchestrated to give interested parties all the information they need so as to understand what is happening, why, and what will be expected of each of them in the implementation of the change. Often, the event must be replicated at different geographic locations. Some companies may choose to use a videotape or video conferencing to conduct the event at different locations. The kickoff event can be supplemented with formal written announcements, electronic transmissions, bulletin board postings, conference calls, etc.

Following the initial announcement, frequent follow-on communications must be made with all concerned. Updates can be most effective if a special vehicle is devised and used for the period of the change. For example, Mobil's REEA departments began an electronic system posting, available to all employees, called REEA Talk to publicize and update everyone on the most up-to-date information about major changes and restructuring.

What have other companies done? IBM's Q&IT organization used town hall meetings, conference calls, and a series of team-building workshops to pass the word and keep people updated. Harley-Davidson hired a professional communications expert to assess what helps and hinders the flow of information; the consultant then coaches and facilitates the organization's managers in improving communications. Attorneys' Title Insurance Fund communicated updates about its culture change via a regularly published newsletter to customers and through an annual assembly where customers come together in a conference environment. The Fund also devoted its 1994 annual report to publicizing the process, results of its culture change, and the accomplishments of its team of employees regarding the culture change (see Exhibit 8-6).

Other publicity strategies at various companies include the use of specially designed novelty items like logos on stationery and forms, coffee mugs, and T-shirts. For example, when discussing a major change at a management retreat, TRW passed out T-shirts with pictures of a dinosaur and a reminder not to become a dinosaur when in the process of change. These novelty items—imprinted with a mission statement, values, or a vision—can be clever ways to communicate a message and provide a constant reminder of what the organization is attempting to accomplish.

Problem-Solving and Innovation Forums

Like all complex processes, the organization culture change is almost guaranteed to go astray from time to time. This part of the model deals with so-called problem-solving forums: mechanisms to bring problems or issues with the culture change process to the surface and to deal with them. You can view such a mechanism as an early warning system to detect unforeseen

Exhibit 8-6. Chairman and president's letter from the Attorneys' Title Insurance Fund 1994 report.

Chairman And President's Letter

Dear Fund Members and Employees:

In past Annual Reports we've talked about change, technology, the future, the past.

This year, at the edge of potentially major changes in the real estate industry, we want to recognize the objectives, the energy, the faces behind one of the significant efforts we've made in recent years — Customer Service Excellence. This Annual Report is a tribute to those Fund employees who made this happen. This report is structured the way our Customer Service Excellence program was — measurement, communication, orientation, and training.

After five years of effort, CSE, as we refer to it, goes beyond a here-today, gone-tomorrow pursuit and is an effort to change our way of doing business. Everyone in the company has been, and will continue to be, trained to meet our expectations in servicing our customers.

The most exciting part of this story is that the entire program was developed by a team of Fund employees — modeling what we hope will be our work organization for the future.

Because that's really what we are facing with CSE and the other changes we will make. There is no question that we — and you in your practices — look different than we did ten or even five years ago. CSE has touched everything we do at The Fund, from how — and whom — we hire, to how we evaluate our performance, how we view and define our customers, how we do our work.

The difficulty in having the kind of good year that The Fund had in 1993 is that it tends to encourage standing pat, to believe all the good things that we see happening and hear people saying.

Our goal is to remain skeptical about what we see and hear; to listen better to all of our customers, both internal and external; to anticipate, prepare for, and lead changes in technology and service — all with the same purpose we've had in front of us for 45 years.

Please join us in the following pages as we celebrate the achievements of the employees of this company, who deserve congratulations for a job well-done.

Sincerely,

Richard W. Lyons
Richard W. Lyons
Chairman

Charles J. Kovaleski
Charles J. Kovaleski
President

obstacles, hindrances, frustrations, or breakdowns that may be preventing progress. If ongoing communication and publicity is the process for the organization to communicate with its constituency, then this mechanism is the process for the constituency to communicate back to the organization. As such, these mechanisms must not just be in place but must encourage everyone in the organization to come forward with issues they wish to be addressed.

This same mechanism should also be an innovation forum, a vehicle for bringing up new ideas and improvements for enhancing the culture change. Fostering input from employees also gives them a stake in the culture change, which will help to ensure their support.

Once issues and ideas have been brought to the surface, you must address and resolve the issues and entertain the ideas. Mechanisms to do so should be visible to the organization and should instill confidence that any matters raised will be addressed fairly, equitably, and with dispatch. Too many organizations elicit feedback from their constituency and then never follow through with action.

As issues are resolved or ideas are implemented, the resolution and/or implementation must be communicated and publicized. When doing so, you must make a clear connection to the problem-solving and innovation forums so that people will continue to use them.

Most organizations have in place some sort of forum for surfacing ideas, but fewer have forums to surface issues or problems. Some are very formal, such as suggestion programs, while others are less so, such as open door policies. Formal programs should be established if they don't already exist.

The U.S. Food and Drug Administration established a tiger team, whose permanently assigned members come together only when a crisis arises. The FDA team gathers information, assesses it, develops strategies, manages the implementation of the strategies, deals with the media, and monitors the crisis through to its resolution.

The advent of Total Quality Management has been the catalyst for many companies to form quality implementation teams to address issues that come up through workforce input. This same forum can easily be used to address culture change issues as they arise. PRC, a large systems integrator company, uses quality implementation teams as a strategy to deal with a variety of issues.

At Attorneys' Title Insurance Fund, each geographically separated branch office established a specific team with the primary purpose of resolving issues with their culture change, or to refer broader organizational issues to the appropriate place. Some organizations proceed less formally, with a standing agenda item for staff meetings to raise ideas or issues and address them.

The senior leadership of the organization must take personal interest in addressing issues raised and entertaining ideas. By taking an active part in these forums, management can take the pulse of the organization and keep abreast of the overall mood and temper.

Ideally, these problem-solving and innovation forums should be established at the outset of the culture change and kept active throughout the process. Many organizations find it useful to continue them into the future.

Accountability

"You get what you reward; you deserve what you tolerate." This adage (attributed to a senior manager at Harley-Davidson) is steeped in truth. The loudest questions heard in an organization undergoing a culture change toward teams are "What will we be accountable for?" and "How will we be held so?" Holding people accountable cements the culture change by ensuring that new cultural and role expectations are met. Feedback from accountability systems gives management data to make decisions concerning promotions, demotions, terminations, pay for performance, and job transfers. The systems that are put in place and what they evaluate then become critical for ensuring success.

Most organizations have some sort of accountability system, usually including an annual performance evaluation and merit compensation program. This means that an adjustment to these existing systems is often all that's needed. For example, the philosophy of teaming that comes out of the Executive Direction phase and the new role expectations arrived at must be integrated into an existing annual performance measurement process as critical factors for evaluation. New behavioral norms, such as sharing information and collaboration as a good team player, may become factors to evaluate in ensuring the success of teams.

When creating a teaming culture within a subculture, it's important to note that the accountability systems set up must operate within the boundaries of the overall organization. Usually, a subelement in a larger company cannot (and should not) create its own performance management system that will use different forms or deviate drastically from the company's.

Let's look at a key aspect of accountability: the individual-versus-team balance. Most organizations weigh more heavily the evaluation of individual performance, and the key to advancement or compensation sometimes relies primarily on individual contribution. A 1993 Conference Board survey found that 75 percent of 382 companies polled provided some form of incentive pay for suggestions or learning new skills—both of which reflect individual contributions. But there is a trend in many companies toward starting to reward everyone more equally.[2] The message, of course, is that we all benefit if the overall organization does well, that is, if we work together as a team.

In a formal teaming culture, team performance and performance on a team must be included in an overall, balanced accountability system. In fact, *The Wall Street Journal* reports, 76 percent of companies engaged in self-directed teams tie member compensation partly to team performance.[3]

When attempting to measure and balance both individual and team performance for accountability purposes, you should consider three areas: results, process, and progress. When evaluating the results of the individual in a team environment, consider such things as fulfilling the contract to the team, the amount of contribution of expertise/effort, the quality of the contribution, and the person's productivity. When evaluating process, consider such things as behavior, degree of participation, and any increase in skills or skill level. Progress can be measured by how well a person is meeting project milestones and by personal improvements.

When evaluating the team's accountability, you can consider results with respect to team success, goal achievement, product quality, customer satisfaction, meeting timelines, and meeting (or beating) financial targets. Team process can be assessed with a view of internal workings of the team (team dynamics), cross-training of members within the team, and use of and adherence to team-based models. To measure team progress, look to performance against milestones.

Organizations are using a great variety of techniques today to hold people accountable for desired performance. Most have found that keeping the process simple yields better results. The usual mechanism is some form of performance review, which can take many paths. Some self-directed work teams use a peer review process (with mixed results), where each team member periodically reviews the performance of other members. Some organizations use customer satisfaction levels as the primary driver for performance review. More and more organizations are experimenting with upward assessments, where team leaders, supervisors, managers, and executives are assessed by their respective subordinates. And many organizations—including IBM's Q&IT—are beginning to utilize 360-degree evaluations, where all of the above have input into individual and/or team performance.

These techniques are carried out in many ways. Surveys are often used for customer and supplier input. Performance review forms of one kind or another are used for traditional management review of employees and sometimes for peer review. Some organizations use independent consultants to conduct interviews (both individual and focused group) to solicit input, especially in upward appraisals of senior managers. Most organizations have some measures against set criteria or standards.

Recent technology developments allow use of automated methods for gathering input into the accountability systems. There now exist ways to make on-line input confidential, and some companies are now using automated input via normal telephone keypads. New methods are no doubt on the horizon.

Mobil's REEA departments implemented a process whereby team members evaluated each other and their team leader. The leader, in turn, evaluated the team members, all against criteria around team process. (Customers and the manager evaluated team results.) The final outcome for the teamwork element was weighted to allow for an increase or decrease of one whole increment on a scale with four possible ratings—clear indication of the importance of teamwork in REEA's culture.

Attorneys' Title Insurance Fund now uses surveys to assess satisfaction levels of both internal and external customers. Managers are then held accountable to show improvement over the next assessment period.

The leader of a subculture can also sometimes implement an accountability system on his or her own. In the Biostatistics and Data Management department at Bristol-Myers Squibb, the director used teamwork as one element in the performance management system, even though the overall company had not yet done so.

The list can go on and on. Suffice it to say that holding people accountable for change to operate in the new culture toward teams is a key requirement if the culture change is to be successful.

Celebrations

The "you get what you reward" adage is certainly not new, and it drives the celebration part of the infrastructure. Celebrations in this context include recognition and rewards, both formal and informal, and celebratory activities for acknowledging success.

Celebrations offer management a way to send a strong message that it is interested in and committed to the organization's culture change. They also are instrumental in helping to shape the new definition of success regarding teamwork. Celebrations motivate the workforce and create incentives for future performance. In addition, positive role models are important in changing behavior toward working in teams. Celebrating positive behavior, both by teams and individuals, is a way to create and perpetuate appreciation of those role models. Rewards and recognition provide the necessary incentives to get people on board the culture change.

As with other systems in the infrastructure, most organizations already have some sort of celebration system in place. These award programs and compensation systems should be scrutinized to ensure that they are designed to promote the behavior desired in the new culture. Most will require some modification—sometimes drastic. IBM's Q&IT, for example, discovered that its entire awards program was geared to the individual contributor. Following the decision to move to a team-based culture, the program was rearranged to include team awards. After one year, 70 percent of the awards given were to teams. This sent a real message to the organization about the importance of teams and teamwork.

Compensation Programs

A change in culture to teams nearly always involves some change in the compensation system. Tying compensation to team performance is usually a drastic move, and it's tricky to accomplish. When adjusting compensation systems, organizations should seek expert advice to ensure that any modifications to existing systems create the desired effect. One organization, for example, created such competition among teams through the compensation system that the newly implemented program had to be scrapped and a new one put in place.

However, when done correctly, compensation to provide incentive for teamwork can be very effective and popular. Organizations use a variety of methods to compensate teamwork. There are pay-for-performance or merit systems, incentive plans under which bonuses are paid for exceeding expectations or meeting stretch objectives, and profit-sharing or gain-sharing plans. When tied to team performance, each can elicit the desired team behavior needed to make the culture change successful.

At IBM, CEO Lou Gerstner changed the compensation system of his senior executive team to make the majority of their overall compensation relate directly to how IBM is faring overall, rather than how their individual divisions are doing. This certainly provides incentive to work as a team to bolster the performance of the entire company. Johnsonville Foods provides bonuses for both individual and team performance that result in increased profits, improved processes, and teaching skills to others. Minnesota's Harzell Manufacturing uses gain sharing as an incentive, where employees receive their base pay plus 50 percent of any productivity increases. Alliant Health Care System pays a bonus of up to $1,200 per team member when his or her team achieves requirements that include such things as having weekly meetings, providing training, and sharing in eleven different team management functions.

Award/Reward Systems

In addition to compensation systems, most organizations have some form of award/reward systems to provide incentive for expected behavior. These too must be assessed for providing incentive for the new behavior required to realize the culture change to teams.

These systems take many shapes and forms. There are monetary-based systems that may include things like vacation or compensatory time off, cash, trips for the team (sometimes including families), savings bonds, gifts or gift certificates, or dinners in an upscale restaurant. Nonmonetary systems might include awards, commendations, public recognition, opportunities to interface with senior executives, free parking, training or cross-training opportunities, or being empowered with greater trust and responsibility. Sometimes these incentives may mean new offices, furniture, and upgraded equipment.

To offer some examples, Attorneys' Title Insurance Fund instituted a program called Going the Extra Mile. Employees "caught" exhibiting behavior supportive of the culture change are presented with a Going the Extra Mile certificate. Each time an employee gets a certificate, his or her name goes into a pool for an annual drawing for some exceptional rewards. The Fund also gives public recognition in a monthly company newsletter in the form of positive anecdotes along with employee names. The accounting firm Peat Marwick encourages interregional and interservice teamwork with a system that rewards business initiation across regions without engendering the severe competition sometimes seen in sales forces. IBM's Q&IT organization sometimes rewards teams for outstanding performance by sending team members and spouses or significant others to New York City for a Broadway play and dinner. Many organizations use team parties, team picnics, or team awards dinners as a way to recognize desired behavior.

The less formal "warm fuzzies" extended by executives are still an excellent method of rewarding team behavior. A pat on the back, a handwritten note, a visit to a team meeting to say thanks can often be more of an incentive than any of the previously mentioned activities. Most people want to meet expectations set by the organization and appreciate being told when they've done so.

Celebrations can also be a way to mark the passing of a milestone in the culture change itself. It's appropriate to celebrate when you meet significant expectations in the culture change plan and realize progress in the journey toward a teaming culture. The celebration in this instance may be a letter or videotape from the senior leader applauding the efforts of everyone. It may be a memento of some sort distributed to everyone to mark the significance of the event. Or it could be a celebratory event such as the one Attorneys' Title Insurance Fund has annually, called CSE (Customer Service Excellence) Day, where employees companywide, in every location, come dressed for the announced theme and share a luncheon, with contests and skits and "speechifying" galore. And a wonderful time is had by all!

After all is said and done, celebrations are a major tool used to provide incentive for the behavior we expect to make the culture change successful. They create a supportive environment that can reinforce the messages from senior leadership that the culture change to teams is important and that it is succeeding.

Discipline and Termination

Probably the most difficult part of the model to exercise is discipline and termination. This is where the organization and its leadership must bite the bullet, where the commitment to change is truly tested. This constitutes the ultimate step in accountability. Once role expectations have been established and communicated, training has been given, forums have been established for problem solving, and accountability assigned, then the organization can expect that all employees and managers will support the culture change to teams. For those who choose not to support it, the remedy should be disciplinary measures, and ultimately termination of employment. This step is neither arbitrary nor vindictive. Everyone must be given every opportunity to succeed in the team culture. But for those who can't or won't, the company must cut the ties.

Again, most organizations have either written or unwritten tolerance levels or criteria for acceptable performance, most often administered by the human resources or personnel department. This part of the model dictates that the criteria or threshold in any policy must be changed to reflect the acceptable boundaries of expected behavior with regard to the new team culture. This step should be taken only in consultation with the human resources or personnel department to ensure that all legal and liability requirements are met.

Why do we recommend this step? The disciplining (or ultimate termination) of wayward employees sends the strongest message to all organization members that this change in culture is real, that it is serious, and that unacceptable behavior will not be tolerated. This is where the rubber meets the road. It is management's test—and you *will* be tested—of the commitment you have to the new culture change and your willingness to follow through with holding people accountable for their performance.

The real key here is the notion that employees and managers in the new team culture must certainly be competent to perform technically in their jobs, but they must also be *compatible* with the new culture.

What does compatibility mean in a teaming environment? It means being willing to share information and resources, putting the team's and organization's goals above your own, and sharing the kudos for success, but also sharing the repercussions for failure. It means being willing to carry your own weight on the team, even carrying a little extra when a teammate is falling behind. And it means being a full participant in the team to ensure that the synergy of the team is optimized.

Unfortunately, in our competitive environment where sometimes only the individual contribution has been revered (and compensated), the switch to being compatible with a team environment can be either very difficult to make or not appreciated as being important. Some refuse to change or are too uncomfortable with the expected behavior. Sometimes the few who refuse to change can intentionally or unintentionally exert enough influence on others in the organization to create a backlash to the culture change. This backlash can easily undermine an entire change effort. Therefore, it cannot be tolerated.

At the outset of the culture change at Attorneys' Title Insurance Fund, two members of the executive team were not in sync with the direction in which the company was moving. They resisted the change and became obstacles to its implementation. The executives were eventually encouraged to retire. Only after their departure was the change implemented and its benefits realized. The Fund has also implemented a probation period for new employees, during which they are evaluated against criteria that include their ability to perform in the new culture. If they are found to be resistant or incompatible, they are let go.

There are numerous examples of new CEOs in organizations who bring in their own teams to ensure that "their" new culture is established. One recent example was Lou Gerstner who, after a honeymoon period, began to replace those on his senior team who he felt would not be able to support or reinforce his new IBM culture. Larry Bossidy at Allied Signal and Ron Sommer at Deutsche Telekom are others who have transferred or terminated executive team members for not meeting expectations.

The true test comes when an employee who may be noted for valuable individual contributions becomes disruptive to the culture change and uses his or her power to undermine the movement to teams. At what point can management no longer tolerate the incompatibility? Is the entire future of the organization worth the contribution of this one employee? IBM has used the term "tyranny of competence" to describe this situation. The tyranny of competence cannot be tolerated if the culture change is to be successful.

The epitome of discipline and termination can perhaps best be shown by the taped message that the CEO of Florida Power and Light sent to all employees announcing the beginning of a major culture change. He used the analogy of a train leaving the station on a journey to a new culture. He emphasized that all were welcome on the train and in fact encouraged to get on. However, if at some point in the journey anyone felt this was not the train for them, or if the company felt this was the wrong train for that person, then there were other trains going other places in other companies where this person might be more welcome and more comfortable.

Notes

1. Judith H. Dorzynski, "Yes, He's Revived Sears. But Can He Reinvent It?" *The New York Times*, January 7, 1996.

2. Peter Nulry, "Incentive Pay Can Be Crippling," *Fortune*, November 13, 1995.

3. Joann S. Lubin, "My Colleague, My Boss," *The Wall Street Journal*, April 12, 1995.

9

Using the Model: Collateral Organizations

When spiderwebs unite, they can tie up a lion.

—Ethiopian proverb

How does your organization go about making the numerous adjustments required in the infrastructure as well as other needs from the Organization Culture Change Model? Obviously the culture change requires a level of effort you may not be able to achieve with your normal day-to-day operations and staff. In that case, a collateral organization (see highlight in Exhibit 9-1) can be very effective. This chapter discusses what collateral organizations are and their role in the culture change process, providing examples of how such organizations have functioned in a number of corporations.

What Is a Collateral Organization?

A collateral organization is a temporary organizational structure put in place to accomplish a specific task. In this case, that task is to help implement the culture change, specifically by working on the Infrastructure and other parts of the Change Model. It is usually in addition to and superimposed upon the normal organization structure.

Exhibit 9-1. The Collateral Organization component of the Organization Culture Change Model.

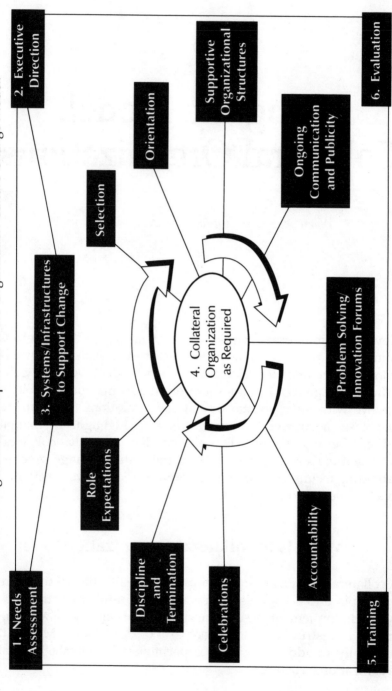

Members are drawn either from various parts of the organization or from an existing group. A collateral organization can be composed of single or multiple groups, which include management and employees at various levels. It should have cross-functional representation when possible and not be given to the human resources department to "own." It is useful to have input from people outside of the systems that need to be changed, which also creates wider ownership.

Members should represent the overall organization as well as provide perspective on their part of the world. They must have credibility and be respected and trusted by others. It is useful to involve informal leaders in this process, along with those who are supportive and willing to partake in a culture change. This does not exclude skeptics, but they must be at least open to considering the change. This is not the time to enlist your biggest naysayers or problem employees in the hope that this experience will change them. There are opportunities to rotate members onto these groups after momentum has been created, and that may be a more appropriate time for adding some of the naysayers.

Making the Decision

The decision to use a collateral organization, and then to decide how many groups there should be or who should participate, depends on a number of factors. Although ideally broader involvement engenders broader support sooner, this is not always realistic or practical. You need to evaluate the size of the organization, the resources available in terms of time and money, the current workload, and the ability or willingness to free people up to work on the culture change. The level of commitment and pressure felt for producing faster results also plays a factor in determining who and how many.

A variety of options have been chosen and work quite well. Attorneys' Title Insurance Fund selected a three-tiered system. It included an expanded executive group (otherwise known as CSEG, for Customer Service Executive Group), a Steering Committee, and four action teams. Delnor Community Hospital in

Geneva, Illinois, formed a cross-functional task force that reported to the executive team. The task force consisted of management and staff and was charged with making the changes. IBM's Q&IT chose to have a subset of the senior management team, otherwise known as the "Culture Club," work on the infrastructure. Its members in turn brought in some ad hoc teams to work on some infrastructure issues, based on need. Mobil Oil's collateral organization was the Manufacturing Team, consisting of senior managers across the research and engineering departments and their business partners, who worked on creating the subculture for the informal organization as well as overcoming obstacles within the existing formal structure and larger culture. First Chicago Corporation used eleven task forces to help implement its merger with NDB Bancorp. Hewlett Packard assigns what they call relationship managers to help manage interrelationships and differences that might arise in joint ventures or alliances. As you can see, there are a number of ways to create a collateral organization whose primary role is to expedite change. The temporary structure provides the extra attention and focus needed, as well as an opportunity for greater involvement and ownership on the part of organizational members in affecting their own culture.

Role of the Temporary Structure

The role of the collateral organization is to assess the various aspects of the Change Model and the systems within the Infrastructure and determine what needs to be accomplished and how best to do that. The collateral organization members utilize the Needs Assessment data that highlight the gaps. In addition, they use the products and decisions that were agreed to during the Executive Direction retreat. Those products include the team-oriented philosophy, goals, Standards for Success, and other organizational direction for the culture change.

The Change Model and Infrastructure framework are used to highlight the systems that need to be worked on, as discussed in Chapter 8. Depending on the structure in place, one or more of the systems are assigned to the collateral organization(s). In some instances, one group would be responsible for all of them. Its role is to create a system that supports the teaming concept, if there is none already in place; to adjust or alter the current system so that it supports teaming; and possibly to eliminate or recommend alternatives to the systems that work against a supportive team culture.

The team or teams are given some guidelines and parameters (discussed later under Implementation) and are expected to fulfill various responsibilities. They are to do any research that may be required, and they are to perform the tasks that need to be done as well as enlist the help of other people or staff functions. For example, when working through the discipline and termination section of the model, one team needed input and help from human resources. In another case, new selection criteria and interview forms were established by one team working with a sample of line managers and employees. The team worked with them on the front end to develop the criteria and forms and later to educate organization members about the new system. So the collateral organization members are also implementors and educators. One team planned and created a new orientation videotape to be used with new employees.

There are instances where the collateral organization members are the decision makers, and other times where they just make recommendations to the most senior or executive group. This depends on the senior leadership's comfort and needs and whether the decisions have broader organizational impact. For example, some ideas on compensation and rewards for teams in one organization needed to be presented to the executive team for approval, as it required reallocation of funds. In another organization, the collateral teams were given constraints within which to work and in turn could make decisions. The level of authority varies in each situation.

One critical role that the collateral teams play is that of ambassador of the culture change. They communicate about what they are working on and why, ask for input, and continually educate about the culture change process. They look for every opportunity to informally talk up what is going on and influence others to get on board.

Organization Support for a Collateral Entity

The temporary structure must be supported by the senior leadership, which needs to agree on the percentage of time collateral team members should work on the culture change, including meetings, conference calls, and individual assignments. A budget should be allocated for travel and the ideas that arise for creating or adjusting the various systems.

The collateral teams must have access to various people at all levels, organizational systems, and associated information in order to make sound decisions. Confidentiality should be expected and ensured. They also need access to either the next level of team up or the senior team, for communicating project status and soliciting input and feedback when needed.

Senior management should be willing to spend some time on the front end in setting up the new collateral teams and defining their direction, expectations, and parameters. Usually this takes only one or two days. Senior management also needs to allocate time to bring the new collateral teams together to ensure an effective orientation process and a smooth start. The teams need to understand what is expected of them, what their role is in the culture change, how they will operate, their deliverables, etc. This orientation—at which they should start their planning—takes an additional one or two days.

Thereafter, the collateral teams need continued support from senior management as well as their own managers (if these are different people) to work on their action plans. Assurance that they can accomplish their assignments during the allotted time is important. Management must also support their attendance at the agreed number of meetings during the year.

Senior management needs to ensure that all organizational members are educated about the informal organization. All managers and employees need to understand why the collateral teams were formed, who is involved, what their mission is, and how they will operate in relation to the formal structure. Continued communication and reinforcement is important. This prevents people from thinking that the collateral teams make up an exclusive secret society. It also paves the way for the teams to enlist input and help from others.

If it is the senior team (or a subset) that is tackling the infrastructure issues, they similarly need to spend time on the front end. In some instances, they may have to come to grips with their feelings of powerlessness and agree to be empowered. This is particularly true when working on their own subculture. They also need to commit to meet and allow time to attend to their expected deliverables. The senior management team must also educate their managers and staff about what they are doing and involve others as much as possible throughout the process.

Implementation

There are numerous strategies you can use when implementing a collateral organization. The approach depends upon the type of informal structure you choose. A multitiered structure requires multilevel planning. That is the alternative we illustrate first, using as an example Attorneys' Title Insurance Fund.

Implementation at the Fund

The Fund selected a multitiered collateral organization for its overall company culture change. It consisted of the Customer Service Executive Group, or CSEG (the executive management team expanded to include a vice-president of human resources and two vice-presidents of operations), a Steering Committee (consisting of middle-level managers), and four action teams (consisting of a wide variety of Fund employees and supervisors from throughout Florida). There were five stages for this collateral organization to become operational, as depicted in Exhibit 9-2.

Stage One: Executive Planning

As part of the Executive Direction retreat, the executive team decided on the collateral structure to be used. They agreed on expanding the executive team to include key operational and staff functions for the collateral organization and identified who might serve on the Steering Committee.

Exhibit 9-2. The implementation stages for the Attorneys' Title
Insurance Fund's Collateral Organization.

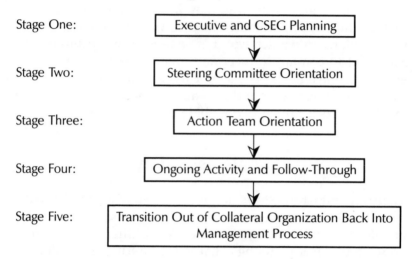

Stage One: **Executive and CSEG Planning**

Stage Two: **Steering Committee Orientation**

Stage Three: **Action Team Orientation**

Stage Four: **Ongoing Activity and Follow-Through**

Stage Five: **Transition Out of Collateral Organization Back Into
               Management Process**

The CSEG had a one-day meeting subsequent to the executive retreat. The purpose was to create better definition of the
roles and parameters of that new structure. At the meeting,
CSEG members decided the role, accountability, and decision-
making authority delegated to each tier. The most senior level
would define the overall direction, intermittently monitor progress of action plans, and have the final approval authority on
the system changes. The Steering Committee would in essence
"steer" the action teams, setting the objectives, serving as a
coach and resource, reviewing work, providing feedback, and
ensuring the communication loop with the CSEG. The action
teams were to develop action plans and do what was necessary
to achieve them.

At that same meeting, the CSEG agreed to the level of support and resources they would commit to the culture change
effort. Members decided to hold quarterly meetings during the
first year, at which all teams came together to work on their
respective assignments. They agreed to have those meetings
once each trimester in years two and three, and semiannually
thereafter until their work was completed. The CSEG also set a
limit on the amount of time per month that action team members would be allowed to work on team assignments, so as not

to jeopardize their other work commitments. The next step during the meeting was to provide some guidance for the other teams' work assignments. The CSEG reviewed each part of the Organization Culture Change Model and the Needs Assessment. They prioritized the various aspects of the model and defined what was needed, including the expected deliverables, guidelines, and constraints for each aspect of the model. For example, under accountability, they specified developing incentive structures that reward organization teamwork and improved customer service. One guideline was that performance appraisals must somehow include that criterion. A constraint they needed to deal with was understanding the budget flexibility for incentive options. For orientation, the need was defined as acquainting new employees with the history, scope of the culture change, and new cultural expectations related to teamwork and customer service. Three guidelines were to define the internal and external customer, what business their customers are in, and what products and services the Fund offers. There were no constraints identified for that part of the model.

Stage Two: Steering Committee Orientation

The second stage was the orientation meeting for the Steering Committee. This served as an educational and role-clarifying session as well as a working session. An overview was given about why the company was embarking on this culture change effort and what the expected outcomes (Standards for Success) were. The committee reviewed the Organization Culture Change Model and how the Fund chose to approach the culture change, including the Collateral Organization. The parameters for changing the culture were shared and included the CSEG's decisions about the collateral structure and various roles and responsibilities, decision-making authority, action-planning requirements, communication and feedback loop expected, and agreements about resources and support for the change effort.

The Steering Committee had the opportunity to interact, ask questions and clarify expectations with the CSEG during the first part of the meeting. It is always important that all members be as comfortable and clear as possible about what is to occur and their role in accomplishing it. This is often an ambiguous time, where things are somewhat cloudy until the team actually goes to work.

The Steering Committee also went through some team building. This helped committee members start off as a high-performing team, short-circuiting any dysfunctional group dynamics. The members applied those skills to the agenda items to be covered. First they identified criteria and selected the action team members, assigning two Steering Committee members per action team as resources. They also agreed on norms among themselves and with the other teams such as how they would communicate, monitor progress, etc. Next, the Steering Committee took the CSEG's broad goals and created more targeted objectives for the action teams, defining how they might help.

Stage Three: Action Team Orientation

The action teams' orientation was the third stage. The same educational and role-clarifying agenda that was followed with the Steering Committee took place for the action teams. There were opportunities to interact with both the CSEG and the Steering Committee throughout the session, which focused on action planning. The action teams developed strategies, deliverables, and time frames. (Exhibit 9-3 shows a sample action plan.) They also delegated individual assignments to work on in between scheduled conference calls or meetings. By the end of the orientation, everyone knew what the next steps were and what he or she was responsible for. In addition, they all had agreed upon intra- and interteam norms for how they would interact.

Stage Four: Ongoing Activity and Follow-Through

Ongoing activity and follow-through was the next phase. It took a number of forms. Individuals worked on assignments, whether researching a subject, generating ideas, interviewing, or soliciting input from others. Each action team and its Steering Committee representative had periodic telephone conference calls. They created minutes to distribute to their own members as well as other teams to keep everyone informed. This was im-

Exhibit 9-3. A sample action plan at the Attorneys' Title Insurance Fund.

Component of the Model: Celebration

Goal Statement: Begin immediately to celebrate significant achievement toward goal attainment of Customer Service Excellence and organization teamwork.

Strategies (What, How, Who Involved)	Responsibilities	Timetable/Milestones
1. Set milestones; determine types of celebrations—individual, group, etc. Identify and set parameters for frequency of celebrations and constraints (budgetary or other).	• Steering Committee (budgetary) • Action Team • Individual Assignments	12/01/88 01/31/89
2. Identify option of publicizing success and celebrations, internal and external.	• Action Team	12/01/88 01/31/89
3. Develop monitoring system and monitor milestone achievement.	• Action Team	01/01/89 12/31/89

portant because a number of systems being worked on were interrelated.

During the first year, the CSEG, action teams, and the Steering Committee came together for two days each quarter for intensive work sessions. In addition, during the two days, the CSEG and the Steering Committee also met independently for half a day each. They worked on their own agenda items and reviewed the action teams' recommendations and products in order to give immediate feedback to them. Although the two-day work sessions were intense, team building and fun were always part of the agenda.

As teams neared completion of their assigned part of the model, they typically integrated their product into the existing environment through an educational or implementation plan. For example, the orientation videotape they had developed became part of the normal orientation process and package for new employees, which was handled by the human resources department. However, the action teams wanted to ensure that all current employees had a chance to see it, so they rotated a copy of the tape to all branches and departments, along with instructions on how to use it with current employees as well as how to reinforce the concepts after a new employee had seen it during orientation.

Some of the implementation plans also included follow-up evaluations to monitor the results and success of the new system, for which vehicles or forms were created. Once an action team met its objectives, the Steering Committee assigned them another part of the model to work on. In subsequent years things got easier for the teams as they grew accustomed to each other, the process, and expected outcomes. They felt more confident and committed to the culture change and their work as they began to see tangible results and get positive feedback.

As an aside: The Fund had to stop financing the project in the middle of this process, as a result of fiscal difficulties. This meant that travel and meetings were on hold, and so was the culture change effort. But the teams were so committed and driven, and the momentum so powerful, that they all elected to keep going and communicate by phone and in writing. Needless to say, the supposed one-year hiatus in the effort turned out to be an extremely productive year.

Stage Five: Transition Out of Collateral Structure Back Into the Management Process

This was the period for transitioning out of the collateral structure and back into the normal organization structure. It involved planning the dissolution of the collateral teams and integrating all of their products, new systems, and evaluation mechanisms into day-to-day operations. Some of the integration had begun already during Stage Four.

Stage Five required each team to recap the new systems created and link them to the appropriate department or part of the organization that would own them. If the systems had not been assigned yet, they needed to identify the owner. In some instances, they identified co-owners of various parts of a product. For example, different departments had to produce reports related to the Standards for Success, with one department pulling it all together. In another instance, they identified a process to alternate responsibility among departments for planning the annual CSE Day to celebrate their successes in teamwork and customer service excellence.

Each team also needed to put together a transition plan that gave some background information and described how to implement the particular system. A transition/orientation meeting was scheduled for the action teams and the department representative who would own the system. Its purpose was to formally hand off the system and help where needed.

The CSEG was so pleased with the results and the metamorphosis they saw occurring that they were concerned about losing momentum without keeping the collateral organization behind it. The CSEG examined a number of options and decided to install a transition team that would consist of members of some of the existing collateral teams. Its members would be responsible for monitoring the environment, making sure the systems were being used and/or were still working, that the results continued, and that people were living the culture. They were to be the pulse of the organization during the transition. The CSEG also decided to stay intact and meet two or three times each year with the transition team on its findings.

The CSEG's and the transition team's roles for monitoring and perpetuating the culture during this transition phase were defined. The roles included what they would monitor and how. It also involved the transition team giving feedback to the CSEG on how they as a senior management group were doing in support of the culture.

As of early 1996, the transition team has been in existence for two years and will continue for now. It rotates members to foster broader involvement and commitment to the changed culture and has been a successful transition for the Fund to its new culture.

Implementation at Other Companies

The five stages described for the Fund can be condensed down to one to three stages in organizations opting for smaller or different collateral structures. The basic goal of each stage is still important, such as executive planning for the collateral organization, orienting whatever entity has been selected, following through to accomplish the tasks required, and making the transition back into the management structure. However, the stages could be simplified or combined.

Let's look at IBM, Q&IT and Mobil as examples that can be compared to the Fund in creating subculture change.

IBM's Q&IT

The Q&IT organization elected to have a subset of the senior management team serve as the collateral organization. Three members volunteered and called themselves the Culture Club. Since they had gone through the Executive Direction retreat, they were well versed on the Change Model and the Needs Assessment results. Their role was to identify the systems that were not in place to support their teaming concept, make the easy adjustments, and form ad hoc teams for the ones that needed more research or ideas. For example, the wording in their awards system had to be adjusted to include team rather than just individual awards—power the Culture Club had, so its members made the change without much fuss. When an orientation package had to be created that described their matrix and teaming concept along with the team culture, the Culture Club called upon three people to pull it together from all of the documents that had been created during the culture change process.

The Culture Club meets intermittently to follow through on various aspects of the model, forming ad hoc teams as needed. The club members report the status of changes back to the full executive group during their regular business meetings. They still have some systems to complete, and they continue to work on them.

Mobil Oil REEA

There were two collateral organizations that evolved within REEA as a method to create improved partnerships between the research and engineering sides as well as with their customers. Both sides had similar missions, to create a new subculture of teamwork and partnership within a broader environment of traditional silos between sections, divisions, and clients.

The first collateral entity was the CADET steering committee. Four middle-level managers from four computer application sections within both research and engineering made up the CADET steering committee. They eventually became affectionately know as the "gang of four" as they overcame their historical conflicts and truly began operating as a solid team. They needed to create a team subculture for the interdisciplinary CADET teams that would function across sections and departments.

At a series of Executive Direction retreats, work began on each part of the model, creating new philosophies, measurements, and role expectations for team leaders, members, etc. The CADET steering committee agreed to a method for holding everyone accountable for fulfilling their roles, tweaking the current performance review. They also resolved accountability issues related to group managers who were part of the formal structure and whose priorities were sometimes at odds. In essence the CADET steering committee completed the necessary changes within the Infrastructure and other parts of the model during this series of meetings. They continued to meet regularly to oversee the teams and the culture change, monitoring the changes and results, and resolving problems that arose. The results were quite positive, and the ideas migrated up to a higher level.

A collateral organization was also formed at the senior management level of the research and engineering sides that included their business partner representative from the Marketing and Refining (M&R) division. It was called the Manufacturing Team and was an important step in bringing the customer as partner into the research and engineering functions. The Manufacturing Team mission was to create a subculture of partnerships for eleven focus teams to manage technologies and customer expectations across divisions. The challenge was similar to but somewhat greater than that of the CADET steering committee since the Manufacturing Team purview had to go across divisions, sections, groups, technologies, and customers.

The Manufacturing Team worked on the culture change during a series of Executive Direction workshops. They made very powerful decisions that affected how their managers functioned on these focus teams, with each other, with their staff, and with their partners. They worked through and completed changes or new systems to create the new subculture. They also continued to meet and monitor the process and culture. They were a success story to the organization and their customers and truly changed how research and engineering worked together in partnership with their customers. This was a prelude to the evolution to one formal organizational entity called the Mobil Technology Company (MTC). It has merged the short-term research and engineering departments to operate in a matrix structure, in partnership with their various customers.

Not Using a Collateral Organization

It is important to note that some organizations choose not to have a collateral organization to facilitate the culture changes. Instead, the senior manager may elect to do it alone (with some coaching) or along with his or her current management team and structure. This can be successful if it fits the circumstances.

For example, the director of Biostatistics and Data Management at Bristol-Myers Squibb chose to work on the infrastructure and other changes with her two direct-report managers. They enlisted help from ad hoc teams to address specific issues such as celebrations and role expectations, making sure that the teams comprised representatives from the two functions plus the two distinct cultures of Bristol-Myers Squibb.

In another case, the vice-president of sales at AMI Semiconductors chose to alter on his own some of the systems related to accountability, incentives, and rewards that were in his sphere of decision making. He also involved his sales managers and sales representatives in a number of the other issues.

Although some organizations choose to use a collateral organization and some do not, the key requirement is that the needed changes to the systems (depicted in the Infrastructure) be addressed to support the culture change.

10

Using the Model: Training

Tell me and I shall forget.
Show me and I may not understand.
Involve me and I shall always remember.

—Native American saying

One of the greatest expenditures of time, effort, and money in organization change strategies has been on training in general and generic team training in particular. We all know that change requires new skills and that employees need to be touched somehow by the change. Training is perceived as a tangible action to accomplish that end. And there are tons of generic team training programs to choose from! These factors have typically propelled organizations into offering generic team training as their primary change strategy rather than actively involving organizational members in the culture change process.

There is no doubt that training is a key strategy for facilitating culture change—but it must be the right kind of training. It must be perceived as an *intervention* rather than just a means of informing or providing skills. And it must be regarded and treated as only *one* strategy rather than *the* strategy. Exhibit 10-1 highlights training in the overall Change Model. Its placement in the model shows its timing. Training is not the first step; rather, it occurs later in the process.

Exhibit 10-1. The Training component of the Organization Culture Change Model.

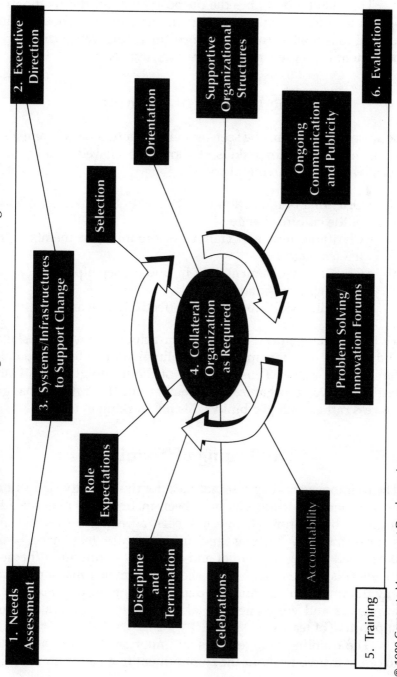

This chapter describes the purpose, content, and methodology for an effective culture change training effort. It should help to maximize the return on your investment and minimize disappointment from the traditional training approach.

The Purpose of Training

Because training must be seen as an intervention rather than just a course for providing skills, it should be viewed as a critical event with the following purposes:

- ▸ Orienting organization members about the why and how of the culture change
- ▸ Clarifying new expectations of organization members in the team culture
- ▸ Creating involvement, buy-in, and ownership
- ▸ Building teams and teamwork
- ▸ Providing skills for working effectively in teams

Once these purposes have been achieved, the team skills and training are then applied to dealing with real team and culture change issues. Thus, the goal of the training session is to begin to involve organization members in the culture change process rather than just build skills for working in teams.

The Timing of Training

The training events begin sometime after the Executive Direction retreat, once key decisions have been made and a plan for addressing the culture change has been agreed on. In some instances the new systems and infrastructure may have been developed during the retreat and are ready to roll out. Whether or not this is the case, having these agreements made prior to any training event is critical in demonstrating the organization's awareness and willingness to take action in creating a culture supportive of teams.

The training then becomes an important kickoff or vehicle to orient everyone about the commitment to a new culture. This also assures participants that they will be stepping back into an organization prepared to support their team efforts. They are also forewarned that the change will not be a sudden metamorphosis but will require time, patience, and their help. The timing and approach of the training event minimizes the classic reaction of most training participants that "this teaming stuff is all well and good, but our bosses and this environment certainly don't support it!" It also maximizes the chances of people buying in and applying the new skills, knowing that the organization will be holding them accountable.

Participation and Sequencing

Everyone in the organization should participate in the training event. If possible, people should attend in intact teams—whether it be a management team, project team, small department, or functional area—along with the team leader or manager. This enables the teams to begin making decisions, applying the concepts together, and planning the next steps. It helps build the team and leads to greater accountability for the change among team members and leaders.

The sequence of participation depends on the organization's size and structure (how many layers, departments, or teams there are). It also depends on what decisions need to be made and by whom, to support the senior leadership's decisions and new directions. For example at IBM's Q&IT, the layer below the senior team was made up of the BALs (Business Area Leaders) and CCMs (Competency Center Managers) who ran the matrix. It was important that they participate prior to others in order to help create the new way of operating. The BALs and CCMs needed to clearly understand the Executive Direction and in turn make decisions on how best to implement the changes. They had to define new roles for themselves and determine how to work in partnership to implement the matrix successfully. They also had to resolve some conflicts and build their team as a role model. The various decisions they made paved the way for subsequent training sessions with the intact teams, each along with the individual BAL and CCM.

The *Fort Lauderdale Sun-Sentinel* rolled out its new decision-making culture level by level, with training of senior editors, department heads, assistant editors, and then staffers. It was important for each respective level to agree on new behaviors, expectations, and action plans accordingly.

At Mobil, following the Manufacturing Team's executive retreat, focus teams participated in the training. They were the next management layer down from the senior leadership team. The focus teams in turn oriented their direct reports. In yet another organization, all the team leaders participated first, and then team members. But the team members did not participate in intact teams because the teams were too fluid for them to affiliate with one particular team. Therefore, team members went through training with their particular skill pool, which was their "home base."

Attorneys' Title Insurance Fund began training with the executive team, then the collateral organization, then the managers, followed by each branch and department with its manager.

The sequence of participation creates opportunities for making decisions and action plans at various levels and then rolling them out during the training. You should consider the following sequence as a framework to use when planning the events:

1. Senior leadership
2. Collateral organization (if one is being used)
3. The next level of management, who are the direct reports to senior leadership (if there is another layer of management)
4. The manager and his or her direct reports, with their intact team or department
5. Intact teams with their leader(s)

Content

The training aspect of the model can cover many topics that support a culture change toward teams. It might include project management, effective facilitation, and meeting management as well as subjects to develop greater technical depth. This section on content deals only with the initial training event rather than such follow-on programs.

The initial training event has numerous components. It defines the Organization Culture Change Model and the Team-Building Model (presented in Chapter 7) as a framework for reviewing the Needs Assessment data, examining the organization's culture, and clarifying the changes to occur. The senior leadership team's Executive Direction decisions and products are rolled out; action plans, new products, and decisions are made by participants in support of them. The Team-Building Model is used throughout the training to build teams and facilitate the team agreements and action plans that will be used in the future by the team. Let's look at each component.

General Culture

In this component of training, participants explore what corporate cultures and subcultures are in general and who creates them. They are asked to reflect on and describe their company's culture and their particular subculture. The various myths about organization culture change are explored. The Organization Culture Change Model is introduced to show how organizations in general can change their culture and how their particular organization has opted to do it. Participants are asked to imagine which parts of the model may show up in the Needs Assessment as requiring adjustment to support their team structure.

The Team-Building Model

Team horror stories are presented and then compared to magical experiences with teams. This stimulates discussion on team/ teamwork myths and ideas about what it takes to be a high-performance team. The critical skills of a high-performance team, illustrated in Exhibit 10-2, are defined. The exhibit displays how the skills must work together just as the gears of a machine mesh. These components were described in depth in Chapter 7.

Exhibit 10-2 is used as a context to receive data feedback on

Exhibit 10-2. The critical components of high-performance teams.

their team that was collected during the Needs Assessment. It also provides the framework for the team building that occurs during the session.

Review of Needs Assessment Data

The data collected during the Needs Assessment phase is reviewed. This includes feedback on the positives and negatives in the current culture's support of teaming and on the strengths and weaknesses of how teams are currently functioning, as well as specific data about the participants' own team(s). Participants are able to see which aspects of the culture and teamwork are to be preserved and which require attention. They do some processing of the data and identify important cultural and team issues for their teams to work on, typically arriving at action plans to resolve them. The team's own data are used as issues to resolve in various exercises throughout the training.

Rollout of Executive Direction Products

The agreements and products that were generated during the Executive Direction retreat are shared, introduced as part of the beginning of the culture change process and the Executive Direction aspect of the model. The products are reviewed and discussed to ensure understanding. Some are used as a stimulus for action planning or decision making. For example, what do teams have to do to influence the Standards for Success? How does the senior leadership's philosophy affect what the teams do or need to do? Teams may also create products or make decisions relevant to their level, such as defining the role of team leaders or members in the new culture.

Team Building

The Team-Building Model (from Chapter 7) is used for developing new team skills while building a high-performing team. The model encompasses the critical components necessary to do so. Since these were discussed in depth in Chapter 7, here they are only briefly summarized:

- ► Clear and agreed-upon goals and objectives
- ► Clear and agreed-upon roles
- ► Optimal use of resources
- ► Effective interpersonal communication, group dynamics, and information sharing
- ► Ability and willingness to confront and resolve conflicts
- ► Effective decision-making and problem-solving skills
- ► Skill in reaching consensus

- Valuing and taking time to be creative
- Sharing of leadership
- Evaluation of process as well as result

The training introduces various skills and techniques for each component of the model. These are then applied to establishing new or improved ways for the team to operate and address real issues. For example, teams are given a technique for resolving conflict, and then they set about dealing with and resolving their internal team conflicts.

Based on some of the data feedback, the teams work on their internal issues (Focus In) as well their interrelationships with the rest of the organization, other teams, and the new culture (Focus Out). Teams make decisions, solve problems, and develop strategies and action plans as they apply the new team skills. Some Focus In issues that teams might address include:

- Establishing or clarifying goals
- Assessing team member expertise and resource utilization, and identifying gaps, overlap, or underutilization
- Negotiating how to better share leadership and responsibility
- Agreeing on what information needs to be shared

Some Focus Out issues that teams might address include:

- Establishing a feedback mechanism with management to ensure that the teams understand and are clear on the same goal
- Agreeing on which other teams they need to interact with and how to do so
- Providing input to the organization about suggested team leader and member roles for the new culture
- Providing suggestions for a contracting mechanism between team leaders and members regarding the expected deliverables and time commitments

How the Focus In and Focus Out issues played out for different organizations can be illustrated through the following examples. Note that the activities and exercises are relevant to each organization and team. Thus, training participants build their team and begin their involvement in the culture change simultaneously.

IBM's Q&IT

During training, IBM's Q&IT needed to understand and work through how a matrix functions and then develop plans for making it operate more smoothly. During Focus Out, participants worked on a contracting mechanism for deliverables and time commitments between team members and leaders. This was important not only for the team but also for the organization's tracking of resources and more effective use of them across Q&IT.

Sample Focus In issues dealt with goals, roles, and leadership. Teams clarified and agreed on their goals. These were forwarded to the senior team to ensure that everyone was in sync and on track about what needed to get done. Teams also worked on assessing their current utilization of member skills to check for over- or underutilization, skills gaps, etc., and identified solutions. They also openly discussed and developed action plans for how they would transition from the traditional leadership and employee styles to the team-oriented style necessary to effectively implement their new structure and culture.

Mobil Oil REEA

During Focus Out, the science and technology focus teams addressed issues related to the infrastructure, key performance indicators, and conflict. They worked on how they would actualize and live within the new infrastructure and subculture. They decided how they would manage and monitor technology across the research and engineering sides along with their business partners, and how they would integrate their staff into the new way of operating. The teams openly discussed the historical conflict and baggage between research and engineering and made commitments for the future. They also agreed on how they would work toward achieving the key performance indicators used as the Standards for Success.

The Focus In areas addressed related to operating norms, communication, and clarifying expertise. The teams agreed on norms for how they would work together and with their staff. They established mechanisms for making decisions, communicating, and evaluating their success. They also identified each team member's expertise and how to capitalize on it, given that they did not fully know each other's expertise based on how they had functioned within the past structure. The teams also assessed which other teams they needed to interact with and how best to do that.

Attorneys' Title Insurance Fund

The Focus Out issues that were addressed by the Fund included strategies for increasing role clarity and interrelationships, improving organization teamwork for customer service, and meeting Standards for Success. They worked on understanding the different roles and interrelationships people had within their own branch, department, and broader environment, and how each of their successes was intertwined with the others'. Teams developed strategies for how they would help influence market share and other Fund Standards for Success. Suggestions were given to senior management for improving overall organization teamwork and customer service.

The Focus In issues at the Fund dealt with defining the customer, living the new philosophy, and empowerment. The teams worked through new paradigms of who the customer is, to include both the internal and external customer. This would be an important issue if they were to actualize the new team culture toward customer service. They also took the Executive Direction philosophy and personalized it in terms of how they were going to live it day-to-day. Empowerment was dealt with and linked to the new philosophy. Managers and employees addressed how they needed to operate differently than in the past.

Team Products

The team products developed during the team building are typed up and used for two purposes after the session. First, the teams use them as their agreed-upon operating norms to live by and action plans to implement. They are a reminder and a road map for their continued high performance. Second, a copy of each team's products is sent to the senior leaders, who review them and provide any necessary feedback. More importantly, the leaders use the products to follow up periodically with the teams and to hold them accountable for following through on their commitments to each other and the culture change.

Teams may also develop products for broader purposes than use by just one team, related to the culture or infrastructure. These are collected from all of the teams at each session and are used by the senior team, collateral organization, or ad hoc team to analyze and come up with a finished product or system to be installed into the new culture.

Methodology

Training methods must be flexible to meet the variety of circumstances within organizations. Following are successful methods used by many companies.

Style and Focus

As should be obvious, the training session is highly participative, with many team and interteam exercises. Simulations are used at times to make a point or have participants step outside of their situations to see a point. Teams are then asked to apply the learning to themselves and make the appropriate agreements or commitments. Their involvement is critical.

Given that team cultures and high-performing teams are mindful of *how* things get done as well as *what*, the team-building aspect of the session focuses on process. In a structured way, teams are asked to stop action in an activity at varying times and evaluate their team process during the activity. They examine their group dynamics, what worked well, and what didn't. The team members then decide how to improve their interaction to better accomplish their goals in the future. They are encouraged to make new mistakes in the next activity, rather than the same ones!

Another aspect of the process that must be observed and dealt with is the overall group's reaction to the teaming structure or culture change. In spite of a realistic and comprehensive approach to the culture change, there will usually be a gamut of reactions during the training events, ranging from ecstatic, supportive, and open-minded to indifferent, skeptical, cynical, annoyed, and outright hostile. Many of the behaviors and perspectives that participants manifest throughout the event reflect the very behaviors and perspectives found in the old culture and traditional styles. The facilitator must be willing and skilled to confront those issues and people in order to move the organization forward.

The emphasis on process heightens team performance as well as preparing team members for a new way of thinking within the team culture. The highest-performing teams are conscious of their dynamics, take time to evaluate their process as well as results, and continue to improve. They are also willing to own their behavior of hanging on to traditional paradigms and to start to let go.

Duration

The training session is usually a two- or three-day event, depending on the individual organization and its needs. Given the intensity of concentration and work required, off-site is recommended.

Facilitation

Who should facilitate the training? There are various options, including external consultants, internal consultants, or a partnership between the two. Very large organizations have sometimes used internal trainers, managers, or employees who have gone through a "train the trainer" program, along with external consultants. The Fund, for example, used external consultants for training the executive team, collateral organization, middle management, and a sampling of employee groups. The external consultants then conducted a train-the-trainer program for ten employees and managers, who learned how to conduct the first sequence of training for the rest of the organization.

Organizations need to be judicious in deciding who should facilitate. They must carefully evaluate the skills of the internal or external people they might use. Culture change requires facilitators who are not only respected but highly skilled in facilitating groups and culture change. They need to be agile and able to deal with the hostility and resistance that will surface during training. The facilitators must also be able to elicit issues and constructively relay them to management.

Involvement of Senior Leadership

It is extremely important to involve senior leadership during these sessions in one way or another. (This does not mean the classic introductory remarks at the opening of the session and then the vanishing act.) There are two strategies that can work very well.

When the size of the organization, time, or logistics are an issue, a panel can be a highly effective way for senior leadership to participate. It requires about two hours of their time per event. Although it is best if all members of the senior leadership attend, it works well to have as many as are available for the various events.

The purpose of the senior leadership panel is to give organization members an opportunity to ask questions, voice concerns, test the senior team members for commitment, and have an open, honest dialogue with them. Therefore, the panel is best held after the orientation about culture change and the rollout of the Executive Direction decisions and products. This gives the groups enough data and fodder for initiating questions and concerns. Since many people are generally hesitant to question their senior managers directly, and particularly so during times of change and insecurity, it is useful to generate the questions in advance. These are then presented anonymously to the panel.

The second strategy involves organizations that are small enough for senior leadership to participate in the session along with their people. With Bristol-Myers Squibb, the department director and both managers participated in the Biostatistics and Data Management Department's team-building event. At the *Fort Lauderdale Sun-Sentinel*, each respective management level attended the particular session where their direct reports were involved. The senior teams presented their decisions and rolled out their products, answering questions and concerns as they went along. Senior leaders were also integrated into the various team building exercises along with the teams.

Regardless of which strategy is used, involving senior leaders is an important statement to the organization. It shows their willingness to commit time, energy, and resources to create a team-oriented culture. It demonstrates their solidarity and teamwork. And last, it sends a very clear message that this is real, not just another training fad.

11

Using the Model: Evaluation

Doubt is not a pleasant condition, but certainty is.

—Voltaire

The Organization Culture Change Model ends appropriately with Evaluation, as shown in Exhibit 11-1. Evaluation measures the results and success of the culture change itself. (Note that, in contrast to evaluation, the "accountability" box in the Infrastructure describes the measurement of performance of individuals and specific teams.)

This chapter discusses how evaluation should be done, with emphasis on the organization's Standards for Success.

Why Is Evaluation Important?

Changing an organization's culture is a complex and difficult undertaking that can take three to five years. For such an effort, it is imperative that measurements be put in place to monitor and track progress. The journey is full of pitfalls, and some yardstick is necessary to ensure that you are on target and accomplishing what you set out to do.

The evaluation process is also a means to show positive

Exhibit 11-1. The Evaluation component of the Organization Culture Change Model.

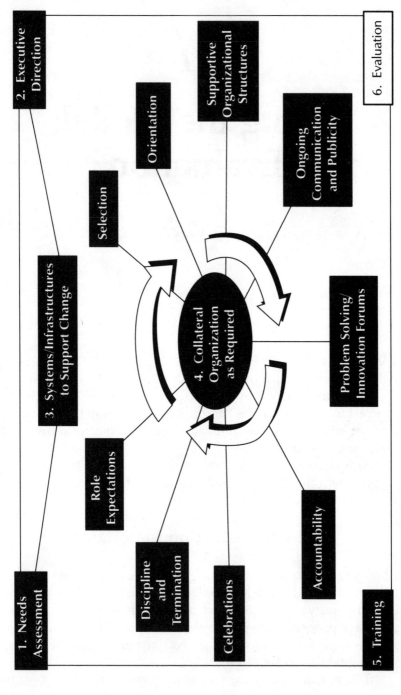

2. Executive Direction

Orientation

Supportive Organizational Structures

Selection

Ongoing Communication and Publicity

3. Systems/Infrastructures to Support Change

4. Collateral Organization as Required

Problem Solving/ Innovation Forums

Role Expectations

Discipline and Termination

Celebrations

Accountability

6. Evaluation

1. Needs Assessment

5. Training

trends that result from the culture change effort. Often, these trends provide the reinforcement needed to convince some in the organization that the change is the correct thing to do. When shared with the workforce, the positive trends tend to help garner buy-in and support. When the naysayers are exposed to data that support the underlying need for the culture change and are bombarded with trends that demonstrate the desired results, they are forced to join the team in support.

The evaluation also provides a way for the organization to hold itself accountable for making the change successful. The organization becomes educated about the culture change through the feedback of measurement data. Members learn where progress has been made and where there is still work to do. This education can be a real motivational tool.

What Is Evaluation?

In the context of our model, evaluation includes the measurement, tracking, and reaction to what we call metrics, established to monitor progress of the culture change to teaming. The metrics, which are linked to the reason for moving to teams in the first place, should measure expected outcomes and in some cases process. The metrics usually measure some organizational indicators of success, including things like product or service quality; internal and external customer satisfaction; financial indicators such as profit, margins, sales, cost of sales, and market share; and personnel-related data such as turnover rates, training, and skill indicators.

Since these measurements are tied to the organization's success, we call them Standards for Success. They differ for each organization. They typically are formulated during the Executive Direction retreat, when each senior leadership team must arrive at its own notion of what to look for as success in its culture change. Each senior team should have no trouble in coming up with a laundry list of things to measure. In fact, the hard part is limiting the list to those things that in fact measure, and provide incentive for, success.

Evaluation should be a measurement of trends over time.

Such monitoring of trends actually guides the reaction of the organization during the culture change transition. The measurements must result in some action taken by the organization in response to the numbers. If a particular trend is moving in the wrong direction, then some action must be taken to correct it. Obviously, if the trends are in the right direction, then the action is to continue on course or even intensify the effort.

Managing the Evaluation Process

As we have seen, during the Needs Assessment process, data are collected regarding what the organization is already measuring and monitoring, and how it's being done. Does the human resources department already keep information on employee turnover rates, employee skills, or what training each employee is scheduled for? Does marketing already keep figures on market share, sales, cost of sales, and so on? Is there an attempt to measure both internal and external customer satisfaction? Typically, organizations do measure some of these indicators.

What does the organization do with the data? Often, there is a huge amount of effort to gather data but the organization never collates the information or reports it in any meaningful way. And if it is collated and reported, it's usually not used to stimulate any action.

At Attorneys' Title Insurance Fund, some branches attempted to gather external customer satisfaction information while other branches didn't. The former did so only sporadically and in a format that was impossible to aggregate to the Fund's overall level. Sometimes the gathered information went into someone's drawer and was never used. Here was a major, expensive effort that served very little purpose.

There may even be problems when the facts are being disseminated. The Fund kept accurate data on market share that were reported to the workforce when market share became one of the company's Standards for Success. However, many in the workforce didn't understand the information and didn't know what to do with it. (The problem was addressed and solved during training.)

Once there is a clear picture of what's being monitored and how it's used, the next step is to use that information in formulating the Standards for Success.

Standards for Success

As the executive team decides what the standards for success will be for the culture change, it must consider what's already being monitored and what's not. Sometimes the organization can stop measuring something if it's not a Standard for Success. Also, some measurements can be combined to give an overall organizational picture. To do so, it's often necessary to dictate some standard format, frequency, and methodology so the data can be accurately aggregated. Let's look at some actual company examples, beginning with the Fund, to examine the use of Standards of Success.

Attorneys' Title Insurance Fund

A case in point is the Fund's effort to measure external and internal customer satisfaction. An action team was assigned to assist in the development of two standard surveys, one to measure external customer satisfaction and the other survey to measure internal customer satisfaction and teamwork. The surveys were then administered annually at the same time. The data were collated and reported to the entire organization and to its external customers. The results were then used to build objectives into the annual performance reviews of employees and managers to ensure that a higher level of customer satisfaction was achieved in the next year. The data were also used in the annual planning process as an organizational accountability tool. As this process was put in place by the action team, the Fund stopped using the multitude of other surveys it had previously distributed. The Standards for Success, including customer satisfaction, used by the Fund are shown in Exhibit 11-2. They are part of the preamble of an annual product produced and distributed to each Fund employee that reflects the company's Standards for Success and the prevailing trends. Exhibit 11-3 shows what the Fund has

Exhibit 11-2. Standards for Success at the Attorneys' Title
Insurance Fund.

The Standards for Success were established to enable us to measure our
progress/success with Customer Service Excellence. If we hit the targets
we've established, and these measurements assess our progress with CSE,
we will have a tangible way to measure our progress with CSE.

The following measurements were established as Standards for Success:
1. **Market Share**—Percentage of title insurance premiums received by
   the Fund in the State of Florida. Measures the Fund's "piece of the
   pie." Obtained from the annual Form 9 (Statutory Financial Statements) filed by the Fund and other title insurers with the Florida Department of Insurance. Preferred trend is upward.
2. **Turnaround Time**—Measurement of what percentage of products are
   delivered to customers by the due date. Benchmark is 95%. Preferred
   trend is upward.
3. **Increase in Internal Customer Satisfaction**—Measurements from
   survey to Fund members to assess employee behaviors and products
   and services from the Fund member's view. Scale is from 1 (completely dissatisfied) to 7 (completely satisfied). Preferred trend is upward.
4. **Increase in External Customer Satisfaction**—Measurements from survey to Fund members to assess employee behaviors and products and
   services from the Fund member's view. Scale is from 1 (completely dissatisfied) to 7 (completely satisfied). Preferred trend is upward.
5. **Certification Date**—Measures the percentage of time the data centers
   meet their service goals. The service goal is a certain amount of time
   after an actual date that the data center is expected to have all applica-
   ble records posted, verified, corrected, and reviewed. Certification
   date may vary by data center depending on how long it takes to get
   the film from the courthouse. Preferred trend is upward.
6. **Personnel Turnover**—Measures the percentage of Fund employees
   who left the Fund during the year. Preferred trend is downward, but
   not too low!
7. **Customer Service Awards**—Measures the number of "Going the
   Extra Mile" awards given during the year. Preferred trend is upward.
8. **Errors Tracked Through Posting Alerts**—Measures errors made by
   the data centers that have been discovered. Preferred trend is downward.
9. **Branch Claims**—Measures claims (in number opened and in dollars)
   that were the result of an error made on a product from a Fund
   branch. Preferred trend is downward.
10. **Bring Back Defectors; Increase Business with Existing Customers**—
    Will be measured by complaints and compliments received on an 800
    Satisfaction Line to be established in 1994 and answered by Finance
    Customer Service personnel.

Exhibit 11-3. The trend in the Attorney's Title Insurance Fund's Standard for success in market share.

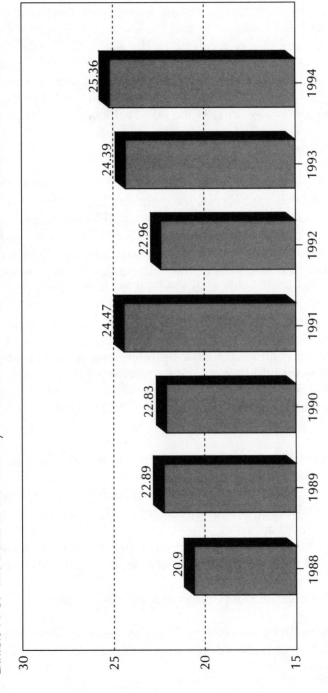

Goal: To increase market share.
Source: Department of Insurance Form 9 Report (June 1995).

done on one of its Standards for Success, market share. It indicates that by 1994 the Fund had more than 25 percent of the title insurance premiums received in the state of Florida. Exhibit 11-4 shows how the Fund has done on another of its Standards for Success, turnaround time on products delivered to customers by the due date. The Fund set its benchmark at 95 percent. As the figure indicates, in 1994 the Fund achieved over 101 percent.

Other Companies

When the executive team in IBM's Q&IT organization considered Standards for Success, the members found that most of the metrics were included in the assessment IBM was already doing as part of the Malcolm Baldrige National Quality Award program. In addition, there are other measurements that are a part of normal IBM life, such as the "Leadership Survey"—a survey that provides all leaders in Q&IT with input from peers and team members—the results of which are now part of the Standards for Success. Q&IT also uses anecdotal data as an indicator of how the culture change is progressing. Independent third parties have conducted follow-up interviews with teams trained through team-building exercises, resulting in qualitative anecdotes that helped the Q&IT executive team to monitor progress.

Standards for Success for Mobil's REEA CADET teams included:

- More satisfied customers in the Marketing and Refining (M&R) division
- The creation of a cross-functional team environment across research and engineering regarding the computer applications area
- Increased savings of staff through economies of scale
- Minimizing conflicts in priorities between teams and the management structure
- Meeting the key performance indicators (KPIs)

When REEA set up its focus teams and Manufacturing Team, the organization drew up new Standards for Success that included such things as:

Exhibit 11-4. The trend in the Attorneys' Title Insurance Fund's Standard for Success in statewide branch turnaround time for products delivered to customers by due date.

Overall for 1992 = 92.48
Overall for 1993 = 93.95
Overall for 1994 = 101.46

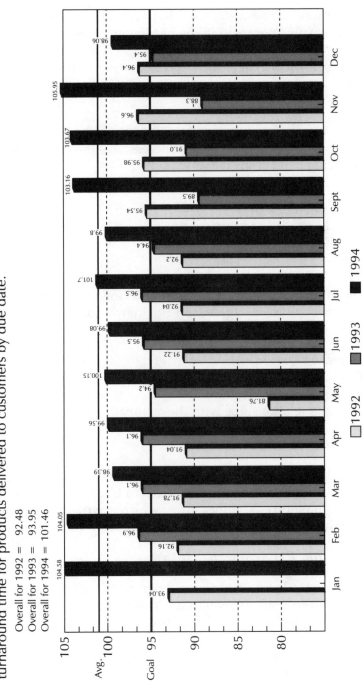

Goal: To provide 95% of products to customers by due date.
January 1993 data not available.
Source: Monthly Branch Service Reports (June 1995).

- Integration of the customer (M&R) into the REEA process
- More involvement within the user community (refineries)
- Better allocation of resources
- Better projects to help the customer
- More implementation of projects
- More migration of projects

Here's one more example. At Gould Semiconductors, the task outlined by the Standards for Success was to create a new manufacturing team culture that would:

- Decrease breakage
- Decrease wafer loss
- Decrease engineer turnover
- Decrease operator turnover

So that his organization could move to a team sales environment, the vice-president of sales and his regional sales directors at AMI Semiconductors agreed on Standards for Success that would:

- Increase sales
- Reduce cost of sales
- Increase communications
- Improve relationships with the factory
- Share commissions
- Resolve conflicts

The list can go on. What's apparent is that each company or organization has devised hard measures to track the success of its changes in culture. The measures, which are determined by the leadership team, are unique to each company and situation.

Collecting and Reporting the Data

Once the Standards for Success are determined and the mechanisms are worked out for what data need to be collected and how, you must decide who collects, collates, and reports the result.

Gathering the data for measurement is sometimes done by the collateral organization. Once the methods and process for doing so are tested and perfected, they are integrated into the normal management process. This was the case at the Fund. There, action teams were assigned the task of turning the Standards for Success into valid measurements, developing methods for collecting and collating the data needed, and then reporting the result to the organization. In some instances (as previously described with the internal and external customer satisfaction surveys), a process had to be developed and implemented. In others, the action teams needed only to identify where the data were already available and extract them.

Once the annual process had been perfected, the methods were integrated into the normal management process; for example, personnel handled the turnover rate, marketing took over the market share and the customer satisfaction surveys, and operations assumed the turnaround time and certification date processes.

When a collateral organization is not used, another part of the organization can be assigned to handle the data, such as finance or human resources. A third party can also be used.

Just a note concerning surveys. Developing and administering surveys requires people with that particular expertise. If you don't have that expertise in-house, you should look for outside help. In some of the cases cited here, the homegrown surveys did not accurately measure what was intended and were sometimes ineffective because of how they were worded.

The evaluation phase is not complete if the data aren't reported to the workforce *and used*. This is how the workforce gets educated and motivated and accountability starts.

Exhibits 11-2, 11-3, and 11-4, presented earlier, are excerpts from the product the Fund uses in this regard. It is an excellent and efficient method of reporting data. As stated earlier in this chapter, the Fund also uses customer satisfaction data in both the annual planning and annual performance review processes to develop action plans to enhance the trends and to hold people accountable for progress. This is also done for measurements such as turnaround time and certification dates. All of this helps everyone in the organization "own" the responsibility to alter his or her behavior to positively affect the trends.

IBM's Q&IT organization reports data in a different way.

The data are collected through the Baldrige Award assessment process and are then reported periodically as the organization is assessed against the quality standards set up for the Baldrige Award. In addition, survey feedback from the IBM "Leadership Survey" is fed back to individual managers in the organization with the expectation that they will take action to improve the numbers over the next year.

Q&IT also reports interim data about the culture change through periodic round tables and town hall meetings held by the vice-president and executive team, with employees. And Q&IT individuals and teams are held accountable for results through the annual 360-degree performance appraisal process.

In Mobil's REEA organization, first the CADET steering committee and later the Manufacturing Team monitored data at periodic meetings and shared the data in reports sent to the various CADET teams and focus teams. The data for REEA's reports were collected through a formal monitoring process set up by an ad hoc team that developed the key performance indicators (KPIs). The KPIs were then passed to a normal management function in REEA that monitored them. Like the Fund, REEA tied results to the annual performance management process.

Another strategy some organizations use is to conduct periodic follow-up sessions to the training sessions. These follow-up sessions are typically conducted by an objective outside group. Their purpose is to revisit the action plans generated during the initial team-building and training session to assess progress. There is also an exercise built into the follow-up to have participants develop a list of successes for the organization regarding teaming since the culture change was begun. Participants also develop action plans for issues that may have arisen since the original session. This provides a forum for problem solving.

The results of the follow-up sessions are reported to the senior leadership team in a follow-up to the Executive Direction retreat. The leadership can then assess the progress of the culture change and make any midcourse corrections necessary for success.

Measuring the progress of the journey through culture change and reporting the results to the workforce provide incentive, motivation, and education to everyone concerning the what and why of their effort. But the real payoff is in *using* the results.

12

Pulling It All Together

Success is not the result of spontaneous combustion. You must set yourself on fire.

—Reggie Leach

This last chapter ties together everything in the book. By now, you should be convinced that to make teams work in your organizational environment, you must engage the concept of culture change. A timeline for implementing the Change Model is provided here to give you some indication of the sequence of events and how much time each event might take.

We also want to close the loop on some of the companies we've used as examples throughout the book and share some of their successes. There is also a word about empowerment and how it can be your key to success. Finally, there are some thoughts about how you as a leader can take the first step and get started in changing the culture in your organization.

Implementing the Model

As previously stated, with diligence the Organization Culture Change Model process can be completed in approximately three years. Exhibit 12-1 lays out the implementation process via a typical sequence of events. Obviously, the length of time for each event and the overall time depend heavily on your organi-

Exhibit 12-1. The sequence of events in implementing the model.

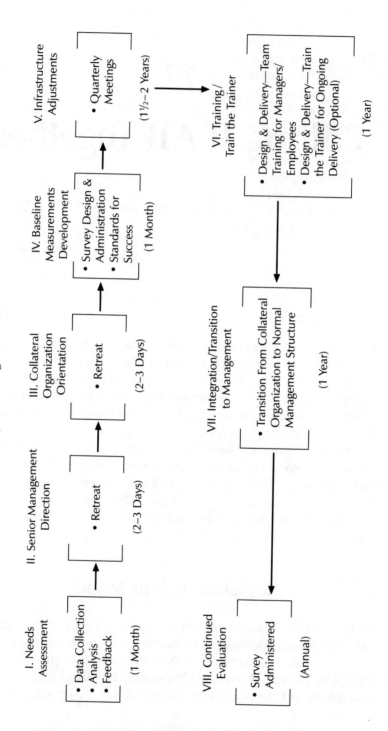

zation's constraints and the results of data gathered during the Needs Assessment. For each event in the figure, there is bracketed information denoting the activities involved, with the typical time it takes to conduct or complete the event given in parentheses.

Exhibit 12-2 gives a timeline from beginning the culture change to the end of year three. As you can see, some events must be sequential; for example, the Needs Assessment (Event I) must precede the Executive Direction (Event II), which in turn must precede the Collateral Organization orientation (Event III). However, there are also many events that may overlap and be completed at the same time. For instance, once the Infrastructure adjustments (Event V) have been started and some progress made (about one year), Training (Event VI) can begin. Evaluation (Event VIII) actually begins after baseline measurements have been developed (Event IV) and is conducted at least annually thereafter.

Closing the Loop

Although numerous companies have been used as examples in these pages, three have been consistently followed through the application of the model. Here is an update on each of the three, and selected others, just to close the loop and let you know where the companies currently stand.

Attorneys' Title Insurance Fund

The Fund, you'll remember, is the largest title insurer in the state of Florida. It is a company that has changed its overall corporate culture. The Fund's goal was to become the best provider of service in its industry within the state and to do so by considering the company as a team and using teams as a vehicle.

The Fund today has continued to increase its market share until it now claims over 25 percent of the title insurance business in Florida. Other Standards for Success trends are heading in the right direction. The Fund has continued to improve its financial

Exhibit 12-2. Timeline for implementing the model.

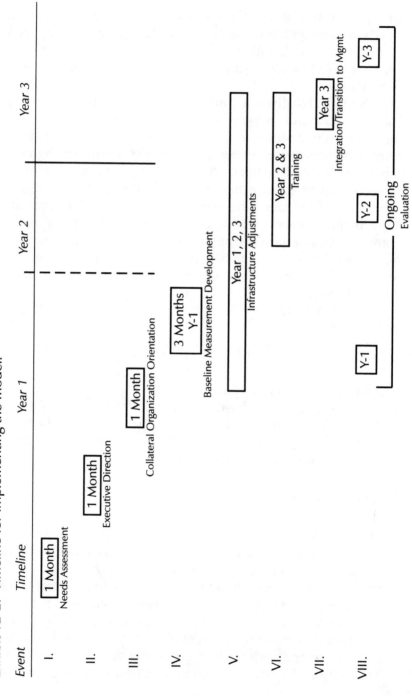

position and has begun to seek opportunities outside Florida. Its story is a major success.

IBM's Q&IT

IBM's Q&IT (Quality and Information Technology) organization, an example of a subculture change, has experienced a number of situations since undertaking its change effort that have affected its progress. Around the one-year point into the change, Q&IT suddenly grew to about three times its original size as a result of acquiring other functions from within the larger IBM. These other functions were not practicing the teaming concept at all or were doing so in different configurations. Absorbing these new functions while maintaining the culture change provided an added challenge. Q&IT regrouped and was making significant headway when another major reorganization hit.

That reorganization transformed Q&IT into the IT (Information Technology) organization. It has dropped back to about its original size, but it has taken on more-varied responsibilities with the addition of a major worldwide role. IT today remains in its teaming structure, albeit with some modifications to meet the new challenges. The organization survives—even thrives—and continues to meet its challenges using teaming as a primary method of operating.

Remember that Q&IT had as a measurement device the Baldrige Award assessment criteria. After its last internal assessment, IBM awarded the organization an internal bronze award for quality. Another major success.

Mobil Oil/REEA

Mobil Oil's Research, Engineering, and Environmental Affairs (REEA) organization, another subculture example, has continued to evolve. It began its effort with the CADET teams, managed by a steering committee. Those efforts were so successful that it went on to broader-based focus teams, managed by the Manufacturing Team. Its latest evolution, to where it is now, was to the Mobil Technology Company (MTC).

MTC was designed as a matrix organization where work on

most projects is accomplished through the joint efforts of so-called core technology personnel (the matrix) along with asset technology personnel. All of this is with the customer as a partner and participant all along the way. REEA's Standards for Success called for better cooperation between the research and engineering sides (which are merged under the MTC configuration) and more customer involvement with the process. In the new configuration, the efforts of MTC are driven by the customer's needs.

Through this evolution to MTC, the organization has maintained excellent work standards and results. And through the use of its team construct, it is doing so with nearly 30 percent fewer people. Yet another success for a company that has undergone a culture change to teams.

Other Companies

Bristol-Myers Squibb's Biostatistics and Data Management Department has rallied to meet ever-increasing demands in productivity. The two functional areas are collaborating much more in their efforts to satisfy their internal customers.

At the *Fort Lauderdale Sun-Sentinel*, the managing editor replaced the vice-president/editor following his retirement. The paper continues to thrive as the highest-circulation newspaper in south Florida and is currently engaged in using teams to implement the latest in newsroom technology.

AMI Semiconductors' sales division has more than tripled sales, from $75 million to $260 million. And in a truly outstanding display of teamwork, when the company allocated half a million dollars as a special incentive to increase wafer fabrication efficiency, the sales representatives committed an additional quarter million dollars of their own commissions as a payout to factory workers when their goals are met.

A Word About Empowerment

Unfortunately, the word *empowerment* has developed a negative connotation in many organizations. However, as a concept empowerment is essential to a successful culture change to teaming. Indeed, teams must be empowered to realize their full potential and be most effective. In an organization that has fewer people and fewer levels of hierarchy, teams must have the authority to conduct their business without undue direction from management.

An even bigger issue regarding empowerment is the notion that leaders and managers with responsibility for their own organizations must *feel empowered* to make change. Too often, we see leaders who are waiting for someone else to direct change. But in an environment where survival is contingent on innovation, flexibility, and quick reaction, we must be empowered to react appropriately. We must understand and seize the power, take risks, and exert control.

Empower means:

- To give strength or authority sufficient for a purpose
- To make able to do something
- To invest with legal power

Given this definition, we must empower ourselves. We must expect and be determined to accomplish what is important. We must feel the power within ourselves to do so. We must be willing to take personal responsibility, action, and risk toward achieving our goal. In our case, that goal must be to change the culture in our organization to support and ensure the success of teams. This is true whether our organization is an entire company with its overall culture or a subunit with its own subculture.

Exhibit 12-3 is the Organization Culture Change Model arrayed as an instrument to assess your degree of control as a leader for your part of the organization. At first blush, some leaders automatically say they have little or no control over some of the components of the model. But usually, after some honest reflection, people realize that they have much more control than they thought at first. For any areas where you don't have control, begin to think of how you can *influence* outcomes. This assessment will be a giant step forward.

Exhibit 12-3. Assessing your degree of control over aspects of the Culture Change Model.

For each aspect of the Change Model, circle C (controllable) or U (uncontrollable) as to whether or not it is within your control to adjust in creating a culture of teamwork.

I.	Assessment	C or U
II.	Management Direction	C or U
III.	Infrastructure	
	1. Role Expectations	C or U
	2. Selection	C or U
	3. Orientation	C or U
	4. Ongoing Communication/Publicity	C or U
	5. Problem Solving/Innovation Forums	C or U
	6. Accountability	C or U
	7. Celebrations/Rewards	C or U
	8. Discipline and Termination	C or U
IV.	Training and Building Teams	C or U
V.	Evaluation	C or U

The Leader's Role

As you and your organization move forward, there are roles that the leaders must fulfill. Your biggest step is becoming aware of the need. Once you've done this, and before you begin your efforts, you should consider the following things when defining the role of the leader and leadership team for a culture change:

1. Clearly define and agree on the new role and behaviors expected of the leadership team to support culture change.
2. Be consistent in sending messages to the organization: what is espoused, practiced, and rewarded.
3. Be aware of and monitor your own behavior and impact.
4. Be aware of your power to influence, both positively and negatively.
5. Be aware of and monitor the culture change.
6. Hold people (including yourself) accountable for change.

7. Continually communicate and educate about the culture change and its progress.
8. Celebrate successes and clearly link them to the new culture.

These considerations should lead you and the leadership team to a set of agreed-on roles to be fulfilled if the culture change is to be successful.

Never forget that you are a role model for the rest of the organization. Exhibit 12-4 depicts in the center column what a good role model should exhibit. The outside columns list behav-

Exhibit 12-4. The leader as role model for creating a new culture.

To Self	Role Model	To Others
Model Behaviors and Systems	Commitment	Reinforce Behaviors and Systems
Reflect	Observe/Analyze Management Behaviors/Impact	Feedback
Receive	Constructive Feedback (Positive and Negative)	Give
Accept	Ownership/ Accountability (Individual and Culture Change)	Reinforce/ Monitor
Identify/Implement Improved Strategies	Effort to Change	Identify/Reinforce Expectations/ Improvements

iors toward self and others associated with each. For example, regarding constructive feedback, you should be willing and able to receive both positive and negative feedback graciously. You should also be willing and able to give the same to others when warranted.

Conclusion

In these pages we have endeavored to present our case that the critical missing link between teams and corporate success is the organizational culture. If you have experienced the disconnection between teams and success, now you know why—and now you know what to do about it to ensure your success. You now have the knowledge and a tool to achieve your goals.

Our topic has been changing culture to support teams, and the Organization Culture Change Model was developed and tested to that end. We have found that the model works equally well with any culture change. May it serve you well in the future.

We find that there are three things required of a leader to be successful in a culture change to teams: awareness, skill, and motivation. Your awareness is your understanding of your own organization's situation and circumstances regarding its culture and the alternatives available. It's also your understanding of yourself and your willingness and readiness to effect change. This book has made you aware of a method, plan, and model for changing.

Skill comes to you through your education and experience as a member, manager, and/or leader of your current or past organization(s). However, sometimes new skills are needed to operate successfully in today's dynamic environment. This book has also provided you with some knowledge and skill in the form of a model to help you be successful.

Motivation can come from external or internal sources. The most powerful motivation comes from within. This book has been an external source of motivation, but hopefully it will stimulate you internally, individually. You must take the first step. Just do it!

Index